Retiring to
Cyprus

Retiring to Cyprus

Pat Yale

Published by Vacation Work,
9 Park End Street, Oxford
www.vacationwork.co.uk

RETIRING TO CYPRUS
by Pat Yale

First edition 2006

ISBN 13: 978-1-85458-362-8
ISBN 10: 1-85458-362-X

Publicity by Charles Cutting

Cover design by mccdesign

Typeset by Vacation Work

Cover photograph: Aphrodite's birthplace, Pissouri

Printed and bound in Italy by Legoprint SpA, Trento

Contents

PART I – BEFORE YOU GO

Housing Finance

PART III – A NEW LIFE IN CYPRUS

Adapting to Your New Life

Quality of Life

Personal Finance

Healthcare

Crime, Security and the Police

Returning Home

FOREWORD

Retiring to Cyprus has always been a dream for thousands of people who have enjoyed idyllic holidays there or have spent part of their working life on the island. Until recently only the wealthy few could afford to turn their dreams into reality but the British house-price boom has had the unanticipated side effect of allowing many people to either downsize to a smaller property and buy a holiday home in Cyprus or sell up altogether and retire to the sun full-time.

For most people this turns out to be a life-enhancing decision that they would never consider reversing. However, before ringing the estate agent and ordering the removals van you should consider one or two things carefully. Cyprus is quite a long way away from the UK which means that it is not as easy (or cheap) to fly back and forth as it is if you move to France or Spain. More importantly although the Republic of Cyprus joined the European Union in 2004 (and the whole island is technically part of the EU), there is still no long-term settlement to the ongoing 'Cyprus problem' which has left the north and south divided into two separate countries for more than 30 years. As a result there are still question marks over the ownership of much of the land, especially in the north. For that reason, if no other, people wanting to buy on the island would be well advised to take good, independent legal advice before parting with their hard-earned cash.

You are unlikely to suffer much culture shock in Cyprus although the north can feel more unfamiliar, especially as it celebrates the festivals of the Islamic calendar which are completely different to those of the Christian one. Although both Greek and Turkish are tricky languages to learn from scratch, especially later in life, most people on the island know at least a bit of English so this shouldn't be too much of a problem.

Another thing to be aware of is the pell-mell speed of development on both sides of the island. Some of the new building is high-quality and attractive but much of it is not and some of it is being thrown up for purely speculative reasons. You will have to choose very carefully to avoid the risk of finding your dream home hemmed in by later buildings that may well obstruct your views.

Amongst the people interviewed during the preparation of this book the other routine grouse was bureaucracy. Whether you are trying to import and register your car, applying for residency or trying to extricate your title deed from the Land Registry Office you are going to need a lot of time and patience whenever it comes to dealing with officialdom.

However, you are highly unlikely to regret moving to Cyprus.

Pat Yale,
Bristol
May 2006

TELEPHONE NUMBERS

Please note that the telephone numbers in this book are written as needed to call that number from inside the same country. Numbers in Southern Cyprus are easy to distinguish from UK numbers because they consist of 8 digits (eg. 8821 3472). However, numbers in Northern Cyprus are easier to confuse with UK numbers because they have 7 numbers (eg. 467 5271). To call these numbers from outside the country you will need to know the relevant access codes.

To call Southern Cyprus from the UK: Dial 00357 and the number given in this book.
To call Northern Cyprus from the UK: Dial 0090-392 and the number given in this book.
To call the UK from Southern or Northern Cyprus: Dial 0044 and the number given in this book minus the first 0.

ACKNOWLEDGEMENTS

Many people were kind enough to let me interrogate them about their house purchases and lifestyle and I greatly appreciate the many lively and informative conversations which almost made me want to move to Cyprus too! In particular this book could not have been written without the help, hospitality and enthusiasm of new Cyprus residents June and Jeremy Hall who told me about life in Lapta and about the Home-Buyers Pressure Group; Deidre Kirk and Nicholas Hugo Vye who filled me in on recent changes in Northern Cyprus; Jennifer Horabin and Bulent Mertgil of Invest and Prosper Properties who explained the procedure for buying a house in the north; Güray Altun who talked me through the recent border changes and what they mean for EU citizens; Graham Colville who enthused about Lefkosia and filled me in on problems for pet owners; Heather O'Brien who advised me on how to shop economically in Pafos; Gina Ghillyer who explained some of the potential pitfalls for newcomers to the island; Sandy Wiley who shared his experiences of building a new house in Polis; and Antigone Louca of the Cyprus Tourism Organisation who pointed me in the direction of many leisure activities I might not otherwise have thought about. Sue Bryant and James Franklin's *Buying a Property in Cyprus* and Nigel Howarth's *Buying a Home in Cyprus* proved especially valuable sources of information for the chapter on buying, renting and restoring property.

Special thanks, to Jim and Lesley Cross, Kim Grand, Alan and Louise Leahy, Kay and Paul Frost and Gill Marcipont for sharing their experiences of life in Cyprus with me. I am also grateful to the users of *www.cyprusliving.org* for some lively discussions especially about problems with timeshare touts.

Part one

Before You Go

Setting the Scene

Basics

Setting the Scene

CHAPTER SUMMARY

- Cyprus is a relatively **easy country to move to** because of its small size and long link with Britain.
- The island is divided into two and where you decide to settle may be taken as a reflection of your **political views**.
- The **warm climate**, with its short winters, is especially appealing to older expats.
- The **cost of living** is lower than in the UK but steadily rising.
- The island may be small but has a wide **variety of landscapes and amenities**.
- It is easy to find **other British expats** anywhere on the island.
- The **slower pace of life** and **low crime rate** are especially appealing to retired people.
- You are unlikely to suffer much **culture shock** in Cyprus although it is wise to gen up on **the island's history** to make sense of what is going on.

THE NEW 'OLD': CHANGING ATTITUDES TO RETIREMENT

At the start of the twenty-first century we are in the midst of a major social transformation. The post-war notion of retirement as a time to put your slippers on and settle in front of the telly with a nice cup of tea is fast becoming obsolete. The very word 'retirement', not to mention the images of encroaching decrepitude that it conjures up, no longer fits the reality of how people are living their lives post full-time employment. Today's retirees are often younger, fitter and wealthier than their forebears and together they are reshaping the very meaning of 'old age' and 'retirement'.

Many social commentators suggest that these changes are being wrought by the baby boomer generation. Born between 1945 and 1965, they are a force to be reckoned with, making up almost a third of the UK population and having responsibility for nearly 80% of all financial wealth. The baby boomers grew up in an era of postwar optimism and new social freedoms, and have always represented a force for social change. Indeed, they have spent a lifetime reconstructing social norms. In 2006 the first of this generation are approaching retirement age, and their political and financial clout means that their approach to growing old is profoundly different. As *The Times* recently put it: *'the pioneers of the consumer society are unlikely to settle for an electric fire and a can of soup'*.

One of the main reasons that the concept of retirement is changing is that people are living far longer. In the 20th century life expectancy rose by 20 years because of better healthcare and greater awareness of the importance of keeping fit and well. Around 18 million people in the UK are over 60. This is creating a crisis for the British economy and, were the government to get its way, we might all be forced to work until we drop, thereby easing the pressure on the over-burdened state pension fund. The new generation of retirees, however, are not prepared to do this. Not only are people living longer but they are also leaving the workforce younger. Many are giving up work in their early fifties when they are still fit and active in order to enjoy a new stage in life – not their 'retirement', according to the American website www.2young2retire.com, but their 'renaissance'.

A recent report by the democracy think tank *Demos* claims that the baby boomers are intent on having their time again; on creating a new life phase in which to revisit their desire for personal fulfilment, free from the pressures of work and childrearing. The report identifies a new 'experience economy' created by peope in search of travel, food, learning and a better lifestyle. The baby boomers don't want to retreat from the world in the way that the word 'retirement' suggests but to head out into it with renewed vigour.

The new retirement is all about finding a better life balance. This may

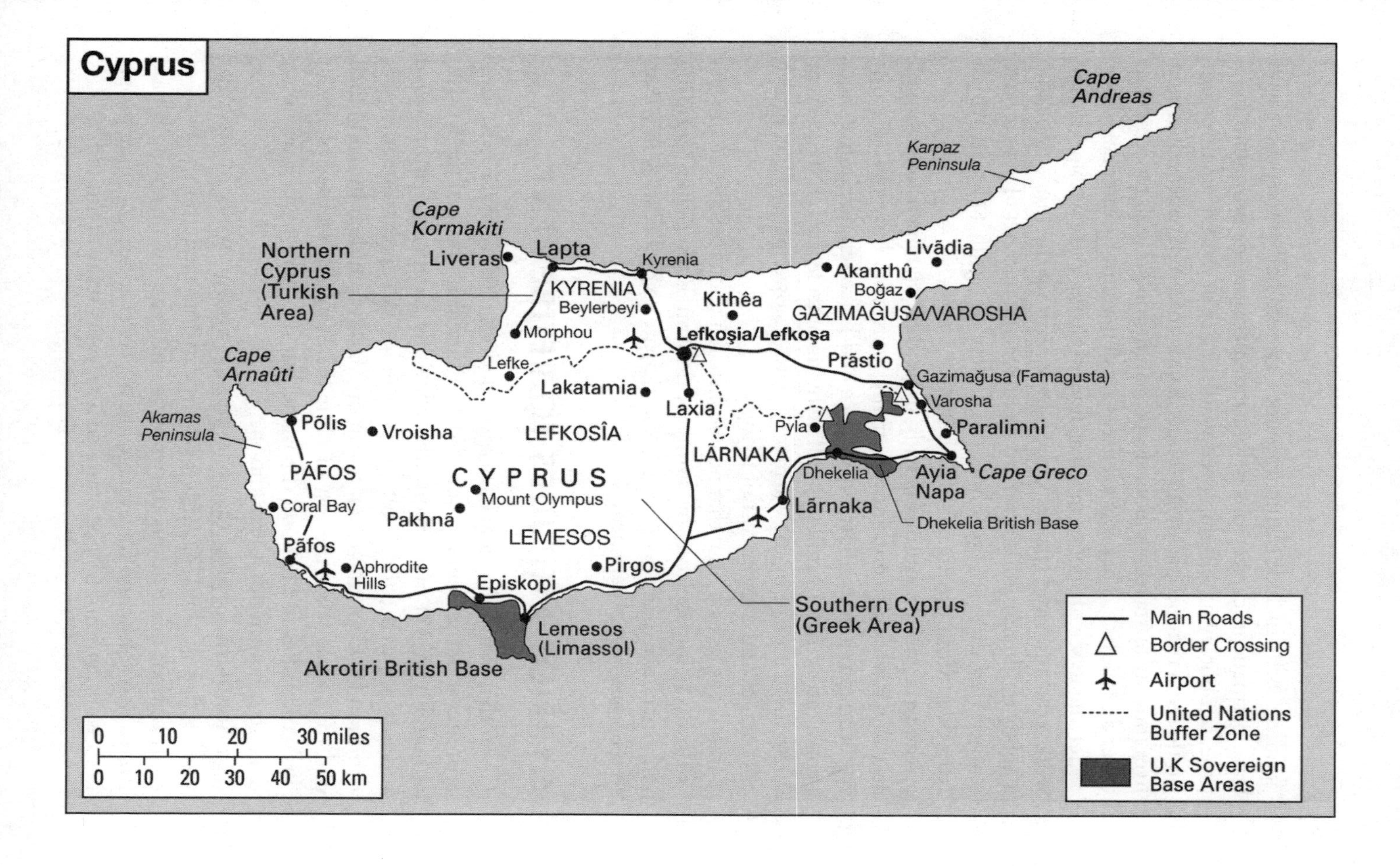
Cyprus
Cape Andreas
Karpaz Peninsula
Cape Kormakiti
Northern Cyprus (Turkish Area)
Liveras
Lapta
Kyrenia
KYRENIA
Beylerbeyi
Morphou
Kithêa
Akanthû
Livādia
Boğaz
GAZIMAĞUSA/VAROSHA
Lefkoşia/Lefkoşa
Prāstio
Cape Arnaûti
Lefke
Lakatamia
Laxia
Gazimağusa (Famagusta)
Varosha
Paralimni
Akamas Peninsula
Pōlis
Vroisha
LEFKOSÎA
Pyla
LĀRNAKA
PĀFOS
CYPRUS
Mount Olympus
Dhekelia
Ayia Napa
Cape Greco
Coral Bay
Pakhnā
Lārnaka
Dhekelia British Base
LEMESOS
Pāfos
Aphrodite Hills
Episkopi
Pirgos
Southern Cyprus (Greek Area)
Lemesos (Limassol)
Akrotiri British Base
0 10 20 30 miles
0 10 20 30 40 50 km
Main Roads
Border Crossing
Airport
United Nations Buffer Zone
U.K Sovereign Base Areas

not necessarily include giving up work – around half of the people who leave permanent 'career' jobs before state pension age move into part-time, temporary or self-employed work, either in the UK or abroad. It would seem that people are no longer happy to compartmentalise their lives into linear stages – school, work, parenthood – with retirement at the end of the line. These days retirees are demanding greater flexibility, preferring to see life not so much as linear but as a cycle with periods of work, education and leisure. Others have built up the funds to pursue a hobby or interest full-time. And an increasing number of people have realised that they can do either one of these things in a climate which frees them from the dreary British winter.

Almost a million Britons already draw their state pensions abroad, and that's without counting the many more who have retired early. According to a new report by Alliance and Leicester, one in five older people (an extra four million) will be living outside the UK by the year 2020, lured abroad by the warmer climate, a slower pace of life, health advantages and a lower cost of living.

It looks as if the gloom that people once felt about the ageing process is slowly being replaced by sunny optimism. Rather than dreading retirement age many people eagerly anticipate a new life stage in which to seek out new experiences.

CYPRIOT ATTITUDES TO RETIREMENT

Given that many Cypriots have spent periods of time in the UK, their attitudes to retirement are not all that different to those of the British, although you will meet many who peevishly complain that only civil servants are well enough off to truly retire. A generation ago it was common for Cypriot women to put on black when their husband died and then wear it for the rest of their life. You will still see plenty of 'little old ladies in black' on the island but it is hard to see their feisty daughters continuing the tradition.

In **Southern Cyprus** the state pension system works in a similar way to that of the UK, with weekly payments made on the basis of contributions made during the working life. Pensions are normally paid from age 65 although the average age of retirement is 63. Some people keep working until 68 but many civil servants retire at around 57.

Although there is also a state pension scheme in **Northern Cyprus** it does not pay very much and many elderly people depend on their family network to support them.

REASONS TO RETIRE TO CYPRUS

When asked why they chose to retire to Cyprus most people immediately mentioned the weather, before going on to comment on the quality of life by which they usually meant the slower pace of day-to-day existence coupled with the low crime rate. Some people also mentioned the friendliness of the Cypriots and the fact that so many of them speak English. A few people commented on the favourable tax regime, with a council tax of perhaps one-twentieth what it is in the UK and a 5% rate of income tax on their pensions. A surprising number of people specifically said that they wanted to get away from a Britain they barely recognised any more – for them Cyprus is a step back in time to many of the things they valued about the UK but now regard as lost; a comfortable country where many locals understand the British way of life and where many things that they think make their lives worth living (including Cadbury's chocolate!) are readily available. Although no one specifically said it, it must help that cars are driven on the same side of the road as in the UK and that everyone uses three-pin plugs just like at home.

Cyprus is very small – the entire population of the island could be dropped into Manchester and still there would be space for newcomers. On the upside this accounts for the slower pace of life and lower crime rate, both things of great importance to people seeking a peaceful retirement. On the other hand the small population (even smaller when you take the division of the island into account) means that it is unable to sustain the range of cultural activities and shopping choices that people from big British cities are used to. The 'British' feel to things could also come to seem a tad dull to people looking for excitement in their retirement.

It has to be said – pell-mell development has left Cyprus, especially the South but increasingly the North too, with some very unsightly buildings. It is also a lot further from the UK than, for example Spain, which means that journeys to and from family entail a longer and more expensive flight than if you were to retire to somewhere nearer home. On other hand a surprising number of people seem to retire here *en famille* which gets around that problem nicely.

Although there is a sprinkling of younger, mainly female settlers who have married Cypriots, in general the foreigners who live in Cyprus tend to be middle-aged or older, reflecting the general tenor of tourism to the island. According to some estimates as many as 80% of foreign residents are from Britain. Around 70,000 foreigners are thought to own properties on the island.

Because of Cyprus's 20th-century history there are a lot of ex-Forces people amongst the retirees. There are also a lot of perennial globetrotters who have worked for the British government in all sorts of corners of the globe, before homing in on Cyprus for their retirement.

Climate. It's hardly surprising that so many people immediately cited the climate as Cyprus' biggest drawcard. The Cyprus Tourism Organisation boasts that the island experiences 330 days of sunshine in a year and has only one month of winter (January). Although it could be accused of being economical with the truth – which is that it still gets pretty cold and wet in winter – it still sounds like a dream come true to people not used to being able to bank on 30 sunshine-filled days in the year.

In high summer it can be insufferably hot, especially inland. However, most foreigners soon learn to take a siesta, snoozing away the hottest part of the day and then getting back down to business when the sun is past its scorching prime.

Health Advantages. The mild climate makes it easier for people to take part in the sort of outdoor activities that encourage good health and it's no surprise to find that Cypriots have one of the longest life expectancies in Europe: male life expectancy averages 76 and female averages 81 (precisely the same as in the UK). Dietary factors encourage fewer cases of heart disease, as does the relaxed way of life and reduced stress levels. Those who are healthy and active when they arrive in Cyprus can therefore hope to remain so for longer. Even those who arrive with minor health complaints find that the climate and calmer way of life help them. Certainly you are likely to fall victim to far fewer coughs and colds than during a typically freezing, damp UK winter. And if you do fall ill Cyprus has some excellent medical facilities.

Cost of Living. While the differential is fast eroding it is still true that Cyprus has a lower cost of living than the UK and it is the things that make life more enjoyable that tend to be cheaper – wine, beer, cigarettes, eating out and leisure activities. The warm climate also means lower heating bills and running a car (if not buying one) is much cheaper because petrol is so much less expensive. However, many of life's necessities are not that much cheaper than in Britain; in particular house prices in Cyprus have been on an upward trajectory for years and in some areas they are becoming prohibitively expensive – the newspapers are already full of stories of islanders who are unable to afford to buy a home. Overall, however, the cost of living may be around 20% lower in Southern Cyprus and 30% lower in Northern Cyprus than in the UK.

Ease of Travel. Getting to and from Cyprus has never been easier (see *Getting There and Away*) despite the absence – so far – of any no-frills airlines and the shortage of ferry routes from Greece. However, it is a four-hour flight from the UK, which could be a disincentive for people who want to be able to fly back and forth between the two countries on a regular basis.

Way of Life. Inevitably the island's small size results in a slower pace of life and people who move to Cyprus tend to rave about how much more relaxed everything is. For those escaping British cities the low crime rate is another plus – it's bliss to be able to park your car without worrying whether it will be there when you return and paradise not to have to shred every document before throwing it away for fear of identity thieves.

British Community. Cyprus' small size means that it doesn't attract as wide a range of British retirees as bigger countries like Spain. Nor does it have the *Under the Tuscan Sun* appeal of countries like Italy which have a clearly defined and relatively homogenous culture. Instead the

British who choose to retire to Cyprus tend to be people who want guaranteed sun and a change from their pre-retirement life but who prefer a relatively small shift of gear in a country which has many other British residents and a broadly familiar lifestyle. No matter whether you live north or south of the *Attila Line* (the border that separates Northern Cyprus and Southern Cyprus) you will have no trouble tuning into a sizeable British community.

Location. Cyprus's position, tucked into the eastern end of the Mediterranean, has a big appeal for some of the people who retire here. As Graham Colville said: '*I feel as if I'm in the middle of things here. I may not actually go anywhere but it's nice to think that Cairo is only a short boat trip away*'. And Gina Ghillyer added: '*It's wonderful to be able to pop across to Beirut to hear Pavarotti!*'

Variety of Scenery. Even though it is so small, Cyprus still manages to pack in all sorts of different landscapes, with a mountain ski resort only hours away from sandy beaches and many walking trails contrasting with town centres that harbour fine medieval monuments.

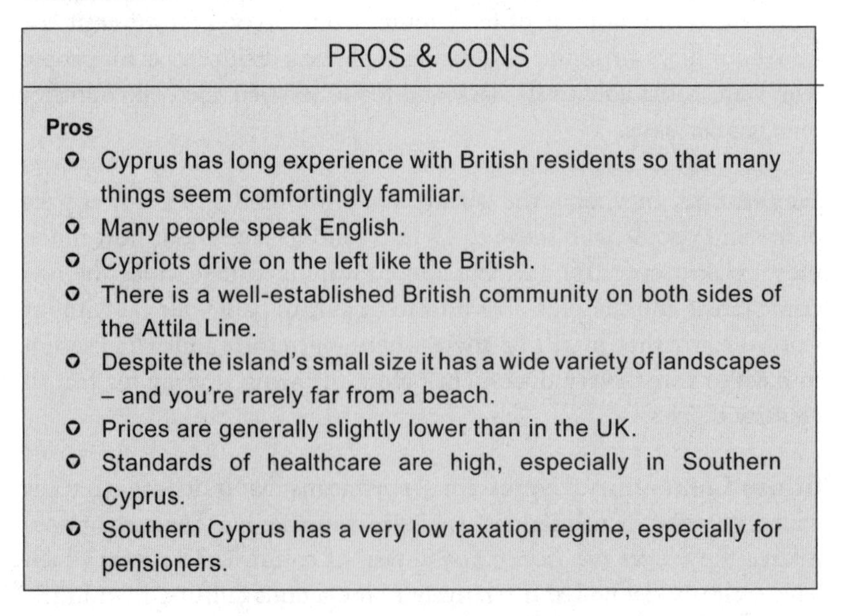

PROS & CONS

Pros

- Cyprus has long experience with British residents so that many things seem comfortingly familiar.
- Many people speak English.
- Cypriots drive on the left like the British.
- There is a well-established British community on both sides of the Attila Line.
- Despite the island's small size it has a wide variety of landscapes – and you're rarely far from a beach.
- Prices are generally slightly lower than in the UK.
- Standards of healthcare are high, especially in Southern Cyprus.
- Southern Cyprus has a very low taxation regime, especially for pensioners.

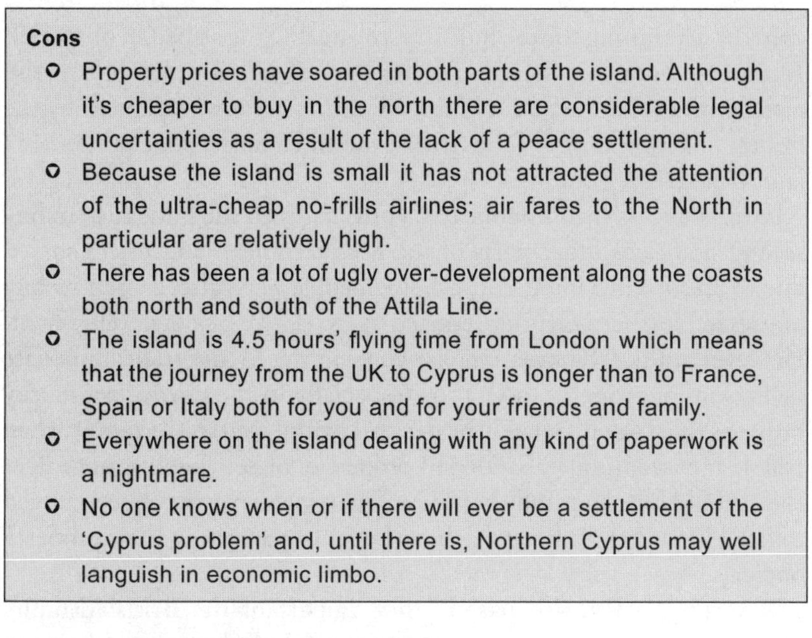

Cons

- Property prices have soared in both parts of the island. Although it's cheaper to buy in the north there are considerable legal uncertainties as a result of the lack of a peace settlement.
- Because the island is small it has not attracted the attention of the ultra-cheap no-frills airlines; air fares to the North in particular are relatively high.
- There has been a lot of ugly over-development along the coasts both north and south of the Attila Line.
- The island is 4.5 hours' flying time from London which means that the journey from the UK to Cyprus is longer than to France, Spain or Italy both for you and for your friends and family.
- Everywhere on the island dealing with any kind of paperwork is a nightmare.
- No one knows when or if there will ever be a settlement of the 'Cyprus problem' and, until there is, Northern Cyprus may well languish in economic limbo.

INTRODUCING CYPRUS

The third largest island in the Mediterranean, Cyprus is squeezed in at the eastern end of it which has given it a strategic importance out of all proportion to its size. Its location also ensures that it has a hot, dry Middle Eastern climate although much of the middle of the island is mountainous and green. The island has two very different communities – the primarily Greek Orthodox community of the south and the Muslim Turkish population of the north. For the last 30 years development on the island has been stymied by the events of 1974 when the Turkish army invaded northern Cyprus to ward off a perceived threat from a military junta which had seized power in Greece and had backed a coup in Cyprus too (see below). The result of the invasion was that the island split into two separate entities, a situation which was set in stone in 1983 when the Turkish Cypriot leader Rauf Denktaş announced the creation of the Turkish Republic of Northern Cyprus (TRNC for short). With the exception of Turkey no other country accepted this division which has left Northern Cyprus in legal limbo.

While the Republic of Cyprus (Southern Cyprus) forged ahead with creating a booming tourist industry, the north languished in obscurity. In one of those disconcerting statements of human inability to rub along with each other, the two communities are now separated by the military paraphernalia of the Attila Line and a buffer zone of no man's land ('the Dead Zone').

In recent years the Republic of Cyprus has seen the same rush to buy second homes as other parts of the Mediterranean and prices soared due to European Union entry. Some people have also chosen to buy houses in Northern Cyprus, seduced by its relative lack of development. However, unlike the situation elsewhere in the Mediterranean, precise ownership of property in Cyprus (especially in the north) is a murky business that may ultimately be decided by the courts. Certainly, when people buy seemingly abandoned properties or seemingly empty land they should bear in mind that the actual owners may have been forced to flee as refugees and may harbour hopes of recovering their property one day.

Nevertheless Cyprus' past history as part of the British Empire gives it a particular appeal to many would-be second-homers. English is widely spoken both north and south of the Attila Line, and people drive on the left as in the UK (although road signs are in kilometres rather than miles). Southern Cyprus is certainly 'Greek' in influence (everyone speaks a local dialect of Greek and the food is certainly Hellenic); however, with its sleepy pace it can sometimes feel reminiscent of the Britain of the 1950s with guaranteed sun thrown in. The north, however, has become increasingly Turkish as more and more island-born Northern Cypriots have left the island, their place taken by settlers from Anatolia who are Turkish through and through.

An estimated 30,000 expatriates live on Cyprus, the vast majority of them British although there are also Irish, German, Dutch and Scandinavian settlers. There are also many residents from Eastern Europe, Sri Lanka and the Philippines. Despite the departure of the British in 1960, the UK still maintains two sovereign bases in Southern Cyprus; Dhekelia on the coast between Larnaka and Ayia Napa, and Akrotiri near Lemesos. The British also continue to use parts of the Akamas Peninsula as a shooting range.

Where am I?

Cyprus' troubled recent history is reflected in its muddled-up place names. In Northern Cyprus old Greek place names have been Turkified. Most importantly Kyrenia has been renamed Girne, Famagusta is now Gazimağusa (Mağusa) and Morphou is Güzelyurt. To further complicate matters, in 1994 place names in the Republic of Cyprus were also changed so that Larnaca became Larnaka, Limassol became Lemesos, and Paphos became Pafos. What was once Nicosia is possibly the most confusing place of all: south of the Attila (Green) Line it is now called Lefkosia, while north of the Line it is called Lefkoşa.

Not everyone accepts these new names and you will quickly become adept at adjusting your words to your audience; calling the port in the north Girne to the Turks and Kyrenia (Kerynia) to the Greeks; describing the capital as Nicosia to older people and Lefkosia to younger ones. However, in this book the new Turkish names have been used for northern towns and villages and the new Greek ones for places in the south. This is not intended to be a political statement so much as an attempt to conform as far as possible with local usage.

As far as the world is concerned Southern Cyprus is officially the Republic of Cyprus (Cyprus for short) while Northern Cyprus is the Turkish Republic of Northern Cyprus, or TRNC. In this book we refer to the two parts of the island either as Southern and Northern Cyprus or as the North and the South.

Introducing the South

If you say that you are retiring to Cyprus most people will probably assume you mean the Republic of Cyprus, the southern two-thirds of the island predominantly occupied by Greek Cypriots. Living here is easier than in the north because, without the economic embargo, the shops are better stocked and systems tend to work more smoothly. Since the Republic joined the EU in 2004 life has brightened up considerably and it must be assumed that it will become easier and easier to find a wide range of imported goods.

Southern Cyprus is where the island's real tourism industry is concentrated and much of the coast was already heavily built up with hotels even before the current building boom brought a rash of new villas and apartment blocks. Most of the older settlements were inland in the foothills of the Troodos Mountains but most of the coastal resorts have a tiny core of older buildings – even Ayia Napa which has a wonderful medieval monastery amid the tacky development.

Most British people have settled in and around Pafos in the south-west, especially since it acquired its own airport. Pafos offers easy access to the undeveloped Akamas Peninsula and to pretty Polis to the north. However, its climate is not just hot but also muggy in high summer, making air-conditioning a must for a comfortable existence. There is also a large British community in and around Lemesos.

Property prices in the south have been rising rapidly and although you can still pick up a derelict village property for around C£20,000, there are also vast mansions on sale for in excess of C£1 million. It is easy to be seduced into equating the Cypriot pound with the sterling pound. However, there is actually a 20% difference in the value of the two pounds – and just how much more expensive some things in the Republic are is likely to become more apparent once it joins the euro zone in 2007 or 2008.

Stanley Morris moved to Paralimni in 1998. When asked why, he cited the health benefits of the climate: '*I have poor circulation and the weather is good for my hands and feet.*' Stanley is typical of many retirees to Southern Cyprus in that he has had a longer and deeper relationship with the island than could come from simply holidaying there: '*I was in the British army here, then in the civil service. I'd lived in Hong Kong and South Africa but it just seemed the obvious place to settle.*' There are many ex-Forces personnel and ex-civil servants living in the Republic.

Charlotte York commented that she had lived in the south long enough '*to see it warts and all.*' For her it is the little things that make retirement there so comfortable – '*small things like having someone fill up your car for you instead of having to do it yourself.*'

Gina Ghillyer runs a very popular bistro in Pafos. She is emphatic about the pleasures of retiring to Cyprus:

> *'You can have the best of both worlds. Here you can enjoy the countryside in the spring. Then in July and August you can go back to the UK to bond with your family because it's too hot here. You can get completely knackered, then come back to nice weather. At Christmas you can either go home again or have your family come here. Then in January and February you can escape the winter by going to somewhere like Egypt or Dubai.'*

Distances in Southern Cyprus are comfortably small; it is only 86km/54m from Lemesos to Lefkosia; 149km/93m from Pafos to Lefkosia; 45km/28m from Larnaka to Lefkosia; and 80km/50m from Ayia Napa to Lefkosia. One of the longest journeys you are likely to make is from Pafos to Paralimni, a whole 179km/111m.

Introducing the North

Northern Cyprus is the part of the island occupied by the Turks in 1974 and declared an independent Turkish Republic by its rulers in 1983. Since then it has become increasingly like a sleepy Turkish backwater town, its high streets adorned with the names of shops familiar from the Turkish mainland, its restaurants serving dishes identical to those in any Turkish lokanta. The Turkish army has also brought with it all the symbols it loves in the homeland: the red Turkish flag fluttering beside the flag of the TRNC and everywhere the cult of Atatürk whose bust or statue adorns every public square.

Because of its illegal status Northern Cyprus has been deprived of development funds since the invasion. Until recently it was kept afloat almost entirely by subsidies from Turkey. However, recently investment has started to come in, some of it from Israel and some, rather quietly, from the European Union via the United Nations Development Programme. The recovery of the Turkish economy over the last few years has had a knock-on effect here too, with Turkish banks and shops opening branches in the main towns. In an encouraging sign that a recovery really is underway a few Turkish Cypriots have started to return to the north with their young families in tow.

So long as the embargo persists the TRNC will be unable to attract the huge numbers of tourists who regularly descend on the South. If anything, the tourism industry is in decline, its place seemingly taken by the construction industry in a sad vicious circle; those people who used to love the North did so for its undeveloped nature and are increasingly put off as cement mixers trundle down country roads and brand-new buildings (or half- buildings) pop up everywhere.

If Cyprus as a whole is small, Northern Cyprus is tiny, its entire population, at around 200,000, less than half that of Bristol. Of that population perhaps 5,000 are expatriates, many of them British retirees. When asked what drew them here most immediately cited the climate, tagging on a liking for the food and the friendliness of the locals. Most still feel perfectly welcome although some suggest that a backlash against foreigners is starting to rear its ugly head, as locals begin to feel themselves 'swamped' by the British as well as the mainland Turks. *'People are friendly but not as friendly as they used to be – there are just so many of us now'* is how one retiree summed it up. On the other hand another said that the British had only themselves to blame if that was indeed the case: *'They don't mix with the locals. They go to British evenings and favoured restaurants that serve English food. They don't make any effort to learn the language and turn up their noses at Turkish food.'* June and Jeremy Hall admitted that the TRNC's smallness could start to feel claustrophobic '*but we can go to the south now, and if the TRNC were eventually recognised our horizons would widen and life would become more exciting.'*

The Compensation Question

The Kofi Annan peace plan put to the vote in 2004 (see below) stipulated that anyone buying a piece of land in Northern Cyprus for which a Greek had a title deed should be paid compensation provided they had started work on developing it. In theory this compensation was to consist of the value of the land in 1974 adjusted f or inflation. The same process was also to apply when someone bought a piece of land in Southern Cyprus for which a Turkish Cypriot held the title deed. The assumption was that this compensation would be paid by the European Union or by the Turkish government and the result was a rush to make a start on buildings in the hopes of profiting from them. However, since the plan was rejected in 2004 there can be no guarantee that the compensation will ever be forthcoming.

The most recent census suggested that more than half the population now live in the urban centres, with 52.8% of the population in Lefkoşa.

Northern Cyprus remains a highly militarised society, with every ferry bringing more young men from Turkey to serve their two years' military service on the island. As a result you will see military paraphernalia – barbed wire fences, notices forbidding photography – even in the depths of the countryside. For some people this would not make for a perfect retirement environment.

Town versus Country

Most Cypriot settlements were built inland during the Middle Ages as a way of protecting them from marauding pirates. In the 20th century the growth of tourism sparked a movement to the coast where most towns are now modern sprawls around a relatively tiny Ottoman-era core. Slowly but surely the inland villages have been depopulated as young people go to school in the towns and never come back; with few opportunities for employment in the villages they have little choice in the matter. The result is that many villages were virtually abandoned by the end of the 20th century; pretty little Phikardou in the Troodos, for example, only has a couple of residents left. The last few years have seen new life returning to the villages at least on a part-time basis as newcomers buy houses there to escape the heat, congestion and noise of the coastal resorts.

A Short History of Cyprus

Because of its political circumstances recent Cypriot history continues to have a direct impact on modern life on the island and on what is and isn't possible there. No would-be settler can afford to turn a blind eye to what has happened since the mid-1950s and especially to what has happened since 1974. It is impossible to understand how the modern Greeks and Turks feel about each other without understanding the long-standing grievances on both sides.

This is not the place for a detailed look at Cypriot history – there are many good books that already do this, including Yiannis Papadakis' recent *Echoes from the Dead Zone*. Below is a short summary of Cyprus's distant history, followed by a more detailed look at recent events which have a direct bearing on the current situation.

Key Dates in Cypriot History

c.6000 BC First settlement of island, probably from Syria or Palestine.

c.1600-1250 BC Bronze Age Cypriots start working copper and trade throughout Eastern Mediterranean area.

c.1250 BC Mycennean refugees and Phoenician traders set up independent city-states on Cyprus. Mycenneans bring cult of Aphrodite to island.

708-663 BC Assyria (Iraq) holds sway over island although city-states retain some autonomy. Cypriots trade with Greek mainland. Royal tombs near Salamis in Northern Cyprus appear to mimic burial practices recorded by Homer.

c.560-540 BC Egyptians take over as Cypriot overlords.

c.540-322 BC As Persia (Iran) becomes more powerful, Cypriot city-states join Greek Ionian Revolt in 500BC. This fails and Persian puppet-rulers take over the city-states.

322-294 BC Alexander the Great defeats the Persians, freeing Cyprus from their domination.

294-58 BC Cyprus is governed by the Ptolemys in Egypt. City-states lose their independence.

59 BC Cyprus becomes part of Roman Empire.

45-6 Christianity introduced to Cyprus by Saints Paul and Barnabas.

115-116 Great Jewish Rebellion. Up to 15% of island's population dies.

330-1191 Cyprus becomes part of Byzantine (Eastern Roman) Empire. From 7th to 10th centuries Arab pirate raids make life on island extremely difficult. From 689 Cyprus is formally neutral and pays tribute to both the Byzantine emperor and the Caliph.

1191 Richard the Lionheart seizes Cyprus and sells it to the Order of Knights Templar. Later he sells it to French Guy de Lusignan as a consolation prize for loss of Jerusualem.

1192-1489 French Lusignan dynasty rules Cyprus. Catholic church becomes more powerful than long-established Orthodox church although Byzantine artists still able to paint the wonderful frescoes in the Troodos churches. Feudal system imposed on island. From 1291 onwards Lusignans become fabulously wealthy on back of passing Crusader trade – Famagusta becomes wealthiest city in Eastern Mediterranean, second only to Constantinople. Traditionally, Lusignans crowned twice – as kings of Cyprus in Nicosia and as kings of Jerusalem in Famagusta.

1349 Black Death wipes out up to a third of the population.

1489 Cyprus ceded to Venetians as result of dynastic marriage.

1571-1878 Island becomes part of Ottoman Empire after bloody conquest by Lale Mustafa Paşa – siege of Famagusta is particularly lengthy and ends with dreadful death of Venetian leader Bragadino who is flayed alive between two pillars that now stand close to old cathedral. Orthodox church regains supremacy, feudal system abolished. Ottomans bring army of settlers from Turkish mainland. Most of old Lusignan aristocracy flee although Church left alone in return for payment of taxes. Several rebellions successfully put down by Ottoman forces.

1878 Congress of Berlin at end of Russo-Turkish War grants Britain the right to administer Cyprus. Greek Cypriots make first demand for union (*enosis)* with Greece.

1914 Britain annexes Cyprus after Turkey sides with Germany in First World War. Secretly offers to give it to Greece if it joins war on Allied side. Greece rejects offer.

1923 Under terms of Treaty of Lausanne, Turkey formally abandons any lingering claim to island.

1925 Cyprus becomes Crown Colony of Britain.

1931 Calls for union with Greece become stronger during Depression. Britain responds by censoring press and deporting 'troublemakers'.

1939-45 Greek and Turkish Cypriots fight with British troops during World War II.

1950 Archbishop Makarios becomes leader of Greek Cypriots. Poll indicates 96% support for *enosis*. Turkish minority – at that time scattered all over the island – become uneasy.

1954 Archbishop Makarios and General Georgios 'Dighenis' Grivas set up EOKA (*Ethniki Organosis Kyprion Agoniston* – the National Organisation of Cypriot Fighters) to try and force British to agree to union with Greece.

1956 In face of IRA-style insurrection, British exile Makarios to Seychelles but can't stop growing calls for independence.

1957 British agree in principle to idea of *enosis*. Shortly after Turkish Cypriots set up TMT (*Türk Mukavemet Teskilati* – Turkish Resistance Organisation) to call for division (*taksim*) of island between Greeks and Turks. Clashes between Greek and Turkish Cypriots and attacks on British. Some of population flee north or south in foretaste of future.

1959 Archbishop Makarios returns to Cyprus. Elected president.

1960 Cyprus wins independence from Britain, with Turkey, Greece and Britain agreeing to safeguard new country's freedom.

The Sovereign Base Areas SBAs)

Two curious leftovers from the days of the British colony are the military bases at Akrotiri, near Lemesos, and Dhekelia, near Paralimni. These two enclaves, covering 158 sq. km of Southern Cypriot territory, are administered by the British military on behalf of the Crown, although they have a customs and currency agreement with Cyprus. You can drive through both areas along the main roads indicated but should not deviate from them and shouldn't take photographs. If you commit a driving offence while within the SBA areas you will be stopped by a British military policeman rather by a Cypriot officer.

Today the two bases are mainly used as listening posts for eavesdropping on the Middle East.

1964 EOKA and TMT resume fighting. Nicosia split along so-called Green Line. British call for assistance in maintaining peace and first UN Forces in Cyprus (UNFICYP) arrive to safeguard Turkish-Cypriot enclaves. US and UN start showing interest in Cyprus; the US in particular regards Makarios as too close to then Communist eastern bloc. Increasingly alarmed, many Turkish Cypriots retreat into self-governing enclaves.

1967 Military junta seizes power in Athens.

1974 Unpopular in Greece itself, Colonels sponsor overthrow of Archbishop Makarios who flees to Britain, then USA. In his place Colonels recognise EOKA-B gunman Nikas Sampson as president. A week later Turks invade north of island, citing their role as guarantors of Cyprus's constitution and need to defend Turkish Cypriot community. Three days after invasion, Colonels order Greek soldiers to invade Turkish Thrace; they refuse, leading to junta's downfall. This is followed by downfall of Sampson on Cyprus. During short ceasefire Glafkos Clerides takes over as president but fighting resumes. In first phase of fighting Turks don't do particularly well, but, reinforced, they bring new vigour to second phase; two days later Turkish army is occupying 38% of island, up to Attila Line. By end of short war, 200,000 northern Greeks have been killed, evacuated or fled south, while 100,000 Turks have been killed, evacuated or fled north. Cyprus left divided in two with Lefkosia, the capital, straddling the divide. New south has lost two towns (Girne and Mağusa), most of its tourism infrastructure and its citrus industry. Arguably north has done much better, acquiring a disproportionate amount of land in relation to its population.

1974 Archbishop Makarios returns to island to start rehousing those left homeless in south. Foreign aid flows in, most of it for south.

MODERN CYPRUS

In 1975 Rauf Denktaş, leader of the northern National Party, announced the creation of the Turkish Federated State of Cyprus and peace talks resumed without success. In 1983 Denktaş announced that Northern Cyprus would henceforth operate as an entirely new country – the Turkish Republic of Northern Cyprus (TRNC) – with its own flag and government. Since then the two communities have lived on opposite sides of the Attila Line which is guarded by United Nations troops. Only in the southern village of Pyla (and to a lesser extent in Potamia) do Turkish and Greek Cypriots still live side by side, albeit using separate tea houses and with a UN watchtower mid-village to make sure they don't start shooting at each other. That this is no impossibility was indicated by events of 1996 when attempts to breach the Attila Line, ostensibly in furtherance of the peace cause, lead to the deaths of several Greek Cypriots and then of several Turks in retaliation.

The 2004 Referendum

In April 2004 the United Nations oversaw a referendum on the Annan Plan, the last attempt to find an enduring solution to the 'Cyprus problem' before the South was due to join the EU. By then Turkey had a new, moderately Islamic government which was hell-bent on joining the European Union itself. As a result the Turkish prime minister Recep Tayyip Erdoğan put pressure on the Turkish Cypriots to accept the plan – which it duly did by a two-thirds majority. Unfortunately with no similar pressure brought to bear on the Greek side of the island the nationalists managed to carry the day by an even more resounding three-quarters of the vote. The inevitable result was that in May 2005 South Cyprus joined the EU on its own. Although the Turkish side won international kudos for agreeing to accept change, other countries have been slow to lift the trade embargo against it. In 2006 it looked as if yet more talks aimed at ending the division would soon take place, once again under UN auspices. In the meantime the only reminder of what happened are the endless '*oxi*' (no) graffiti still defacing walls in the south.

In 2004 the Republic of Cyprus (the south) joined the European Union, with the Turkish Republic of Northern Cyprus left out in the cold. In theory the entire island has joined the EU. However, EU law is suspended in the north until such time as a settlement can be concluded. As soon as it had joined the EU Southern Cyprus started to demand that its ships and planes be allowed to enter Turkey. Turkey responded by saying that this was impossible until the EU lifted the embargo against Northern Cyprus. Although the Turkish Republic of Northern Cyprus is still unrecognised by the UN, in 2005 the USA gave it $10 million as part of a $30.5 million project known as the Cyprus Partnership for Economic Growth which aims to bring the two sides closer together. The EU has also given money to UNDP (the United Nations Development Project) for environmental improvements in Girne and Mağusa. However, the stalemate continued into 2006 and looked like becoming a sticking point in EU negotiations with Turkey. In February 2006 a Greek Cypriot ship attempted to dock at Mersin in Turkey, claiming a right to do so as a result of Turkey's Customs Union agreement with the EU. Inevitably, it was refused permission to unload.

The Republic of Cyprus has joined the European Exchange Rate

Mechanism and is expected to start using the euro in 2008. For the time being the Cypriot pound (C£) remains in use but the Republic is expected to introduce dual Cyprus pound/euro pricing in the next year or so. The Turkish Republic of Northern Cyprus uses the new Turkish lira (YTL), the currency of mainland Turkey. A hangover from the link with Turkey is that you will still hear islanders talking in 'millions' of lira – this is because until the new lira was introduced in 2005, the old lira had become worth so little that it took almost 2.5 million lira to buy one English pound!

The Current Governments of Cyprus

Southern Cyprus. Under the Southern Cypriot system of government the president is both head of state and of the government (i.e. there is no prime minister). The president is elected every five years, on a different date from parliamentary elections to the 56-seat House of Representatives. The current president/prime minister is Tassos Papadopoulos.

Northern Cyprus. Northern Cyprus also has a presidential system of government and far fewer signs of real democracy. Despite five-yearly elections Rauf Denktaş remained president from the declaration of Northern Cypriot independence until 2005 when he was finally replaced by Mehmet Ali Talat. The UN continues to deny legitimacy to the TRNC so he is usually described as the 'representative of the north' at international forums.

The assembly of Northern Cyrus has 50 seats. In theory Northern Cyprus also has 24 seats in the House of Representatives although they have not been filled since 1963.

The Cypriot Economy

Southern Cyprus. The Southern Cypriot economy has boomed on the back of the tourism industry, with more than 2.7 million tourists holidaying there every year. Few stretches of the south coast are free of high-rise hotels but Southern Cyprus attracts everyone from middle-aged British birdwatchers to youthful sun, sea and sex-seekers.

In all, 75% of the Cypriot economy is taken up by the service industry, predominantly tourism which accounts for 20% of GDP. However, Southern Cyprus also earns money from exporting fruit, vegetables, wine and fruit juice and from a small shipping industry. It also has a thriving industry offering health services to visitors from the Middle East. Other industries include cement and gypsum production and ship repairs. Only 4% of the population work in the agricultural sector which produces olives, grapes, citrus fruits, vegetables and barley.

Northern Cyprus. In contrast Northern Cyprus has languished in economic limbo, attracting fewer than 50,000 tourists a year. Nor does it have any really successful industries; those it does have have been stymied by Greek pressure on other nations to boycott goods from the north. Not surprisingly, many of its most able young people have left in search of a better life elsewhere, leaving the country even more dependent on support from the Turkish Republic. The difference between the two sides of the island is illustrated by the stark figures for exports: while Southern Cyprus exported goods worth $1,094 billion in 2005, Northern Cyprus could only manage exports worth $49.3 million.

At the time of writing two of the North's more successful ventures were the construction industry and education, with new universities, including a flash new branch of Ankara's Middle East Technical University (METU – Ortadoğu Teknik Üniversitesi), opening to meet the demand.

Divided Loyalties

Perhaps it would just about be possible to live in an expat enclave near Pafos and never have to think about the division of Cyprus. However, for most people the reality is that the sad legacy of the 20th century will rarely be far away from any conversation with local islanders, and where you choose to live will usually be taken as a statement of which side you support, whether you want it to be or not.

Population

Although no census of the whole island has been taken since 1960, the Cypriot population is assumed to consist of around 800,000 people, of whom perhaps 600,000 are Greek Cypriots. The last census taken in the north concluded that there were 198,215 residents; of these, perhaps 75,000 were actually settlers from mainland Turkey who had taken the place of indigenous Turkish Cypriots as they left in search of a better life elsewhere; another 20,000 are students and 30,000 are soldiers which means that the Turkish population of the island probably exceeds the Turkish Cypriot one. Although many Greek Cypriots who fled in 1974 have chosen to return to live in Cyprus again, it is only in the last few years that Turkish Cypriots have started to return to live in the north

Only around 400 Greek Cypriots remain in Northern Cyprus, mostly on the Karpaz Peninsula. There are also around 140 Maronite Christians still living on the Koruçam Peninsula. Perhaps 3,000 Turkish Cypriots continue to live in the south.

The growing expat community, much of it British, is mostly concentrated along the coast and in a few inland villages.

The Cypriot Diaspora

One consequence of Cyprus's troubled 20th-century history is that many Cypriots from both sides of the island have left, with many of them heading for the UK. At the time of writing there were thought to be around 300,000 Cypriots living in the UK, many of them in North London. On top of the UK residents there are also around 4,000 Cypriot students in the UK. As a result it is hard to spend any time on the island without bumping into people who live in the UK – indeed who may turn out to be close neighbours – for most of the year. Turkish Cypriots, in particular, have left the island in huge numbers as the embargo against the north stymied prospects there. If a settlement is ever reached some may return. In the meantime some of the 'Brits' retiring to Cyprus turn out to be Cypriots returning home at the end of their working life.

Geography

A mere 90 km south of the Turkish port of Taşucu, Cyprus resembles a sheepskin laid out flat with its neck facing towards the junction of Turkey and Syria. A vast plain – the Mesaoira – is squeezed in between the limestone Kyrenia Mountains of Northern Cyprus (also known as the Beşparmak Dağları in Turkish, the Pentadaktylos in Greek and the

Five-Fingered Mountains in English) and the igneous Troodos Mountains of Southern Cyprus with the Cypriot capital Lefkosia/Lefkoşa in the middle of it. Most tourism development in the south has taken place along the flat land between the Troodos and the sea. The least-developed part of the island is the Karpaz Peninsula (called Karpasia by the Greeks), the neck of the sheepskin pointing to the north-east, although the Akamas Peninsula and the Tylliria region in the south are also still fairly undeveloped. At 1951m, Mount Olympos is the highest point on the island and plays host to a small skiing industry.

Cyprus covers 9,250 sq. km in total and is divided into two with 68% of the land mass making up the Republic of Cyprus and 32% making up the Turkish Republic of Northern Cyprus. The island has a 648km coastline.

Climate

One of Cyprus's biggest selling points is that it has at least 300 sunny days in the year. The entire island has a typically Mediterranean climate, with hot, dry summers alternating with cooler, wetter winters and very little in between. The Troodos Mountains see snow in winter and temperatures there can fall below freezing. Most of the rain falls in autumn and winter.

When thinking about retiring to Cyprus it's important not to underestimate the sheer intensity of the summer sun. While most people like the outdoor lifestyle that comes with warmer weather older people in particular can find extremes of temperature hard to cope with – and the heat of July and August in Cyprus is extreme by most people's standards. It is made worse in some areas by high humidity; Pafos, for example, is humid even in early summer.

From mid-July to mid-September it would be unusual if any rain fell on the island.

Weather Forecasts. To find out what the weather has in store for you in Southern Cyprus tune into CyBC2 (FM91.1MhZ) after the news at 10am, 2pm and 8pm daily. There is also a weather forecast on CyBC TV2 every evening after the 9pm news. Otherwise, the *Cyprus Mail* or the Cytanet website (www.cytanet.com.cy) should do the job.

AVERAGE MAXIMUM TEMPERATURES				
Area	**Jan**	**Apr**	**Aug**	**Nov**
Girne (Kyrenia)	17C	23C	36C	23C
Lefkosia	15C	24C	37C	22C
Lemesos	13C	23C	37C	21C
Platres	8C	20C	30C	15C

CULTURE SHOCK

Cyprus is an easy country to visit, with little risk of extreme culture shock. This is especially true of the south where long acquaintance with the British, followed by long experience with tourism, has knocked edges off the Greekness. Language is the most overt symbol of a Hellenic background, but so many people speak English that even that is rarely a problem.

The north is a harder nut to crack especially as more settlers arrive from economically-deprived parts of Turkey. But even there many people speak English and there is a general familiarity with the ways of the west. The one exception, perhaps surprisingly, is Lefkoşa which feels increasingly like a slice of back-of-beyond Turkey.

National Character. Ironically, given their considerable differences, Greek and Turkish Cypriots share many characteristics. For both groups family is extremely important and for both a woman's chastity used to be an absolute imperative. As time has passed, such characteristics have started to soften on both sides of the Attila Line. However, while Southern Cyprus is now far more relaxed and liberal, Northern Cyprus is arguably becoming less so as more and more settlers from rural Turkey have moved in.

The Family and Attitudes to Women. Traditionally Cyprus was a very conservative island in which both Christians and Muslims laid great emphasis on the family as the focal point of life. A woman's chastity went along with this – it was the basis on which families were built up and women who strayed were viewed with disgust on both sides. The impact of tourism on the south in particular has undermined some of the importance of family and young Greek Cypriots may seem not very different from their northern European counterparts; certainly a woman's virginity at marriage is no longer the be all and end all of life. However, economic isolation means that tourism has not had such a profound impact on the north where traditional Turkish reverence for the family is still largely intact. Since many of the more recent settlers have come from poorer, less educated groups in Turkey they have brought with them their own less forgiving attitudes to women's behaviour.

The Siesta. For many people it comes as a surprise to discover the siesta alive and well in Cyprus, especially in the south. Perhaps it shouldn't be that surprising, given the extraordinary heat of high summer. Still, in an age of air conditioning it can seem like a throwback to times past to find banks and post offices closed throughout the early afternoon in the south, especially as in the north they tend to work a more conventional 8am to 5pm day.

Alcohol. Alcohol is readily available all over Cyprus and even in the north you are unlikely to have problems with it – the Turks who come to live in Cyprus are not usually fundamentalists.

Relationships. As with alcohol, so with sex. The Cypriots have seen it all, and although they are tiring of the drunken antics of the British in Ayia Napa, they are not about to suggest that their visitors rush to the altar before they can stay together in a hotel room. Traditionally, though, the Cypriots have kept a close eye on the 'honour' of their own women; both communities have insisted that women be virgins on marriage while turning a blind eye to the rovings of their men.

Homosexuality. Neither the Greek nor the Turkish Cypriots are keen on homosexuality. It is not actually illegal in either part of the island. However, open displays of homosexual affection in public are not going to go down well.

Nightlife. Almost all the nightlife on Cyprus is currently concentrated in the south where resorts like Ayia Napa have given Ibiza and Falaraki a run for their money in the 18-30 party-crowd market. In Northern Cyprus only Girne (Kyrenia) makes even a stab at late night revelry. You'll see nightclubs littering the roads out of town but most of them are aimed straight at the Turkish military market and don't have much to offer expatriate Brits.

Basics

CHAPTER SUMMARY

- The **cost of living is lower** in Northern Cyprus than in the south but is rising fast all over the island.
- Instead of buying a permanent home in Cyprus you could consider **renting** there or **buying a holiday home** and letting it out for part of the year.
- To be sure you really want to make the move it is wise to **spend an extended period of time** on the island first.
- Few expats **learn Greek or Turkish** although if you do make the effort it will enrich your new life considerably.
- Everything to do with **extending visas, acquiring residency, taking out citizenship**, etc is likely to take a frustratingly long time.
- There are many more options for **flying** to Southern Cyprus than to the North. Now that the border is open for EU citizens, people living in the North can make use of flights to and from the South.
- **Pets** can be imported into Southern Cyprus from another EU country without having to go into quarantine. This is not the case with the TRNC.
- Provided you have residency, you can import all your **household effects** into either part of Cyprus duty-free.

THINGS TO CONSIDER

Is it Affordable?

Of course it's easy when sitting at home on a cold January afternoon to dream of the Cypriot sun and decide that you would like to sell up and retire to the island. However, the one thing that is certain about any decision to move to a different country is that the more you have thought everything through, the more likely it is that things will work out well in your new life.

One of the first things you must consider is whether you can afford to make the move. While it's true that Northern Cyprus is cheaper than the UK, prices have been rising fast there, and life in Southern Cyprus is not necessarily all that much cheaper than in the UK, especially if you take into account the cost of regular flights home. In particular the cost of land and property has risen dramatically and there are now properties on sale in Southern Cyprus for in excess of C£1 million.

UK Retirement Pension Forecast

If you have not yet reached retirement age but plan to start receiving your UK state pension in Cyprus you should continue to pay national insurance contributions in the UK in order to qualify for a state pension once you reach 65. You should also request a Retirement Pension Forecast. This tells you the amount of state pension you have already earned and the amount you can expect to receive upon reaching pension age, which will help you plan your finances for the future. To receive a forecast, obtain Form BR19 from your local social security office or contact the Retirement Pension Forecasting and Advice Unit: ☎0845-3000 168.

Cypriot Cost of Living Compared with the UK

There is a considerable difference in the cost of living between the north and south. In **Southern Cyprus** prices are comparable to those in the UK; indeed, they can sometimes be higher, a difference which will become more apparent once shopkeepers start using the euro. Typically a couple might need to budget about £60 a week just for food. However, inflation is only around 2.3% annually.

In underdeveloped **Northern Cyprus** prices are about 30% lower than in the UK, although not as cheap as on the Turkish mainland.

Alcohol			
Product	**UK price (£)**	**Price in Northern Cyprus YTL/£ sterling equivalent**	**Price in Southern Cyprus C£/£ sterling equivalent**
Table wine (750 ml)	4.99	7.00/3.00	3.30/4.00
Beer – known brand (330 ml)	0.92	1.60/0.70	0.46/0.56
Scotch (6 yrs old – 700 ml)	12.34	39.00/6.75	13.59/16.55

Cars			
Product	**UK price (£)**	**Price in Northern Cyprus YTL/£ sterling equivalent**	**Price in Southern Cyprus C£/£ sterling equivalent**
New low-priced car (900 -1299 cc.)	8,995	14,000/6,000	5,900.00/7,195
Unleaded petrol (1 litre)	0.95	1.55/0.66	0.55/0.67

Electronics			
Product	**UK price (£)**	**Price in Northern Cyprus YTL/£ sterling equivalent**	**Price in Southern Cyprus C£/£ sterling equivalent**
Personal computer	941	15,900/6,850	799.00/974.00
Colour television (66 cm)	498.98	700.00/300.00	190.00/230.00
Basic mobile phone	39.99	50.00/21.50	30.00/36.50

Food			
Product	**UK price (£)**	**Price in Northern Cyprus YTL/£ sterling equivalent**	**Price in Southern Cyprus C£/£ sterling equivalent**
Milk (1 litre)	0.49	1.30/0.55	0.60/0.73
Eggs (12)	1.02	2.50/1.10	1.19/1.45
Orange juice (1 litre)	1.22	1.40/0.60	0.91/1.10
Butter (500g)	1.96	5.20/2.25	1.00/1.20
White bread (loaf)	0.55	0.80/0.35	0.75/0.90
Tea bags (50 bags)	0.30	4.65/1.99	1.61/1.96
Fresh chicken (1 kg)	1.7	2.80/1.20	2.29/2.79
Potatoes (2 kg)	1.50	3.00/1.28	0.60/0.73
Onions (1 kg)	0.64	0.85/0.35	1.00/1.20

Healthcare

Product	UK price (£)	Price in Northern Cyprus YTL/£ sterling equivalent	Price in Southern Cyprus C£/£ sterling equivalent
Routine check-up at family doctor	85	40.00/17.00	25.00/30.50
X-ray at doctor's surgery or hospital	45	20.00/9.00	25.00/30.50
Aspirins (16 tablets)	3.99	7.50/3.20	0.66/0.80

Leisure

Product	UK price (£)	Price in Northern Cyprus YTL/£ sterling equivalent	Price in Southern Cyprus C£/£ sterling equivalent
Cinema seat	6.50	10.00/4.30	4.00/4.85
3-course dinner at good restaurant	40	30.00/12.90	20.00/24.00
Compact disc album	11.99	4.00/1.75	9.99/12.20

Newspapers and Magazines

Product	UK price (£)	Price in Northern Cyprus YTL/£ sterling equivalent	Price in Southern Cyprus C£/£ sterling equivalent
Daily English-language newspaper	0.60	1.00/0.42	0.55/0.65
Imported daily newspaper	1.20	3.75/1.60	1.60/1.95
International weekly news magazine (*Time*)	2.60	4.50/1.95	2.60/3.20

Rents

Product	UK price: London (£)	Price in Northern Cyprus YTL/£ sterling equivalent	Price in Southern Cyprus C£/£ sterling equivalent
Furnished moderate 1-bedroom apartment (pcm)	600	250.00/105.00	200.00/245.00
Furnished moderate 3-bedroom house (pcm)	1200	450.00/195.00	350.00/425.00

Tobacco			
Product	**UK price (£)**	**Price in Northern Cyprus YTL/£ sterling equivalent**	**Price in Southern Cyprus C£/£ sterling equivalent**
Cigarettes – Marlboro (20)	5.20	3.90/1.65	2.25/2.75
Cigarettes – local brand (20)	4.77	1.50/0.65	1.65/2.00

Utilities			
Product	**UK price (£)**	**Price in Northern Cyprus YTL/£ sterling equivalent**	**Price in Southern Cyprus C£/£ sterling equivalent**
Phone line – average monthly rental	10.66	6.00/2.55	7.95/9.75
Electricity – monthly bill for two	40	35.00/15.00	80.00/34.35
Water – monthly bill for two	30	23.00/10.00	10.00/4.30

What you pay for items like clothes and shoes depends on personal taste. It is probably fair to say that prices for such items are much the same as in the UK although it is perhaps a little harder to find cheap T-shirts, underwear etc. on the island.

Tourist Prices. One of the more frustrating aspects of moving to a country with a large tourist industry is that goods in many seemingly ordinary shops are already marked up to prices it is assumed tourists are willing to pay. Even in shops where this is not the case some owners will up the price as soon as a non-Cypriot walks through the door and it can take a long time to establish yourself as a local in their eyes. This is less likely to be a problem in a village where there are fewer tourists and where the shopkeeper will accept you as an honorary local more quickly. To avoid paying over the odds it makes sense to do most of your shopping in supermarkets where prices are clearly marked and apply equally to everybody.

Leaving Family and Friends

When thinking about quitting the UK people sometimes underestimate the strength of the ties that bind them. Moving abroad inevitably means that you will see less of family and friends – and the further you move, the longer the gaps are likely to be. For people with grandchildren in particular it can be hard to realise that they are going to miss out on things like first steps, first words and early birthdays. These days computers equipped with webcams and software that makes it possible to make cheap phone calls, have made it easier to keep in touch with people back home. However, there can never be any real substitute for physical proximity.

Most people realise how much they will miss their family but omit to take into account that they will also be giving up a social network developed over a lifetime. If you have been visiting Cyprus on a regular basis you may have built up an alternative social life there which you think will compensate. But there is rarely anything to compare with an old friend, especially when times are hard.

Women often feel the separation more than men and for some homesickness can have a seriously detrimental effect on the new life in Cyprus. You will need contingency plans to stay in touch with elderly parents, friends and other relatives, and to deal with any emergencies that may arise in the UK while you are away.

Bear in mind that some relationships may not survive the separation. You may think you know your friends so well that nothing could damage your relationship but sometimes physical distance results in emotional distance too. Some people simply can't be bothered keeping in touch by e-mail or other remote means. Some may be jealous of your new life, others simply confused and disappointed by your decision to move away. Only time will tell.

Can I Face the Disruption?

You will need great reservoirs of energy and enthusiasm to deal with your move both practically and emotionally. Many people cite moving house in the UK as one of the most stressful times in their life, even though that move doesn't involve flying to another country, isolating yourself from friends and family, and having to take onboard an unfamiliar culture. The first few weeks in your new home may feel very strange, however well you thought you knew and loved Cyprus. You may even have days when you wonder what you have done. Try and make allowances for this emotional confusion – usually it will be over in no time at all and you will be out on your verandah soaking up the sun and wondering why you didn't make the move sooner.

Looking Ahead

Many people retire when they are still relatively young and healthy, and prefer not to think about the implications of moving abroad and jettisoning their normal support network just as health problems are likely to start cropping up. Cyprus has high standards of medical care but you need to think about whether you will be able to cope there as you get older. In particular you need to think about what would happen if you become seriously ill or are no longer able to care for yourself. The family unit is so much tighter in Cyprus that there has not been a need for nursing homes and personal home care services. Social and economic developments in Cyprus may eventually force change but for the time being the infrastructure is insufficient to cope with a growing population of dependent elderly people. This is very important, especially as the UK government is considering ways of enforcing the rule that people who have lived abroad for more than three months are not immediately eligible for free NHS care upon returning to the UK.

If you have moved to Cyprus with a spouse or partner, you also need to consider what will happen if one of you dies or becomes seriously ill. Research suggests that such events can quickly lead to a crisis as newly-created social support networks prove less effective than having family and long-time friends close to hand. In the case of bereavement the surviving partner may not want to stay on in Cyprus, and you need to consider that possibility before deciding to sever all links with the UK tax and national insurance system. It can be extremely difficult to slot back into the British system once you have left it.

If you're thinking of retiring to Northern Cyprus it is also important to consider what the future may bring in terms of a political settlement. Before buying property in the North it is vital to check its ownership status; some of the land that has been sold in the North arguably belongs to Greek Cypriots who were driven from their homes and may eventually return to them as part of a peace settlement and vice versa. You should not assume that people who have bought the land in the meantime will automatically be compensated.

ALTERNATIVES TO PERMANENT RETIREMENT IN CYPRUS

For most British people it is almost knee-jerk instinct to assume they will buy a house in the country to which they are retiring. However, it is at least worth considering the alternatives. Someone selling their house in the UK and investing the money carefully might be able to rent for many years while retaining the possibility of moving elsewhere or even returning to the UK should they so wish.

Living in Cyprus will not be for everybody and there are several advantages to keeping your UK property and taking extended holidays there instead. Retirees are able to take holidays during the low season and school terms when prices are lower and the resorts quieter. For years some British tourists/expatriates have been wintering in Cyprus, thereby avoiding the heating bills and cold weather back home. Some of them own a holiday home, but others enjoy extended rentals or take advantage of timeshare and home-exchange deals.

The obvious advantage of the last three of these alternatives is that it relieves you of the worry of buying and maintaining your own property. Not owning a property also frees you to spend your extended holidays getting to know new parts of the country better.

Holiday Homes. It is perfectly possible to buy a holiday home in Cyprus and spend part but not all the year there. If you do this you can try and let your house for the rest of the year, and so bring in a small rental income to top up your pension. There are a couple of potential snags with this rosy scenario. In the first places as Cypriot property prices have soared it is not as easy as it once was to buy a second home there without selling your house in the UK to finance the purchase. Secondly, as more and more people have piled into the Cypriot buy-to-let market, so it is becoming harder to find people wanting to rent all the available properties, certainly for an income that would make having them in your house worthwhile.

Timeshare. Timesharing allows you to buy a set period of time at a property every year for a set period without having to own it for the whole year (in effect you share it with lots of other owners). In theory you can swap your timeshare weeks with timeshare owners elsewhere in the world, thus enabling you to take your holidays in other countries. In Cyprus timeshare properties are mostly sold around Pafos which is where you are most likely to be approached by a tout. Cypriot law allows for a 15-day 'cooling off' period in which you can pull out of a contract signed too hastily. However, by far the best advice is to proceed with extreme caution and only go to look at timeshare properties if that is what you were thinking of doing *before* anyone approached you to do so.

Timeshares have had a bad reputation in the past so make sure you do your research before buying and try not to be taken in by high-pressure sales tactics. EU regulations on timeshare sales stipulate that you must be given a 'cooling off' period, allowing you to pull out of a contract before any monies are paid. Remember that contracts must be printed in the mother tongue of the prospective purchaser (i.e. in English if you are English or Irish) and should spell out the sellers' identity and address, all the costs involved, the location and description of the property, and the number of weeks in the year that you can use it. You need to know what management fees must be paid as these can bump up the apparent price considerably. For further advice contact the Timeshare Consumers Association (☎01909-591100; 24hr advice line: 0901-607 0077; www.timeshare.org.uk).

Leaseback. Leaseback arrangements allow you to buy a property from a developer at a reduced price in return for which the property is leased back to the developer for a set number of years. The developer then takes on the cost of furnishing, managing and maintaining the property over the lease period as well as renting it out to holidaymakers. The purchaser retains the right to use the property for a set number of weeks in the year and continues to be its registered owner.

- Leaseback arrangements are more likely to be available for upmarket properties
- Leaseback makes sense if you have capital to invest in a property but are not in a hurry to become a full-time Cypriot resident.

Extended Rentals. There is nothing to stop you renting a home for as long or short a time as you want. Although some people regard money spent on rent as wasted others would argue that rents are relatively cheap in comparison with buying and that saying no to the temptation to invest in bricks and mortar enables you to stay footloose and fancy free.

Many companies rent out holiday properties at a reduced price during the winter. This may not be much use to you if you want to stay put for a long time as the rental period will expire at the end of the low season. However, for many retirees this is ideal – they can escape the gloomy British winter and return home just in time for spring.

- Holiday rentals are normally charged on a weekly basis, with anything longer than a month constituting an extended rental. Some companies only rent for up to three months at a time but others will consider a year.
- Major tour operators such as *Thomson* (www.thomson-holidays.com), *MyTravel* (www.mytravel.com) and *First Choice* (www.firstchoice.co.uk) offer such longer-term holidays, marketing them particularly to an older clentele.

Useful Contacts

Holiday-Rentals.com Ltd: ☎ 020-8743 5577; www.holiday-rentals.com.

Cyprus Villas: ☎ 2466 5408; www.cyprus-villas.com.

Villarama: www.villarama.com.

Home Exchanges. The idea of swapping homes as a way of taking a cheap holiday started in the late 1950s, and recently it has undergone a revival on the back of the internet revolution. Home exchange websites advertise thousands of homes worldwide and offer instant communication and virtual tours to help you make up your mind. If you have an inviting house in the UK you might want to consider signing up to a home exchange scheme and swapping with someone living in Cyprus. Alternatively, if you have an attractive house in Cyprus you could try swapping that with people living elsewhere. In theory this would allow you to retire to Cyprus while also having the chance to spend periods of time, rent-free, in other countries.

- House swapping gives you the chance to get to know a particular area and decide if you would like to buy your own property there.
- Many house-swap arrangements include swapping cars and pets.
- Usually both parties continue to pay their own utility bills, community charges, mortgage repayments etc.
- Most agencies charge an annual fee of around £65-115 to advertise your home.
- House and contents insurance policies may cover home exchanges but read the small print carefully.

Exchange Agencies

Homelink International (UK): ☎01962-886882; www.homelink.org.uk.

Intervac Home Exchange: ☎01249-461101; www.intervac.co.uk.

A TRIAL PERIOD

There will always be people who decide on the spur of the moment to up sticks and retire to Cyprus. The temptation can be enormous, especially when confronted by the grey drizzle and dark evenings of a British winter after returning from a blissfully sunny two-week holiday. However, such a life-changing decision should never be taken lightly and many people who rush into retirement abroad find that the grass is not necessarily greener overseas to their great disappointment. Many people miss their family and friends, feel cut off by cultural differences or simply find economic inactivity boring. Even if you know an area really well, your romanticised notion of retirement to Cyprus may not quite live up to reality.

The best way to make sure that you are making the right decision is to spend an extended period of time in Cyprus before making the final decision. You may think that you have already holidayed there so many times that you know what you are doing but being on holiday and actually living somewhere are completely different things. Most people can manage to survive any number of holidays abroad without hiccoughs. However, humdrum daily life anywhere is always going to be a bit of a rollercoaster and as soon as you make that big move your life in Cyprus will become as subject to the normal ups and downs of daily life as it was in the UK.

A trial period can take the form of one prolonged stay in a favourite place or it can consist of several separate reconnaissance trips to different areas that you think you might like. Ideally, you should stay in the area that you most fancy for long enough to get to know what makes it tick. In particular, you should be sure to spend a winter there because many areas undergo a complete character transformation in the off-season; it would be a shame to find yourself living in a virtual ghost town in winter when you had assumed you would have company all year round.

Although you could take an extended holiday in one of the hotels that offer cheap winter rates it's much better to rent a property near where you think you might like to live. Try and rent something similar to what you want to buy so that you can find out not only what normal life is like in your chosen area but also what problems can occur with particular types of property. You might, for example, find that you would prefer to live further away from the main resorts or that Cypriot village life isn't going to suit you. Alternatively you might find that a villa with a pool or large garden is going to require more maintenance than you are prepared to give it.

Settling somewhere temporarily also gives you the chance to start getting to know the locals and making friends. Crucially, it also gives you a chance to tap into the local grapevine and start finding out the real going rate for properties, and who are the most reliable estate agents and tradespeople. You can also use the reconnaissance period to work on your Greek or Turkish so that you are ready to handle dealing with bureaucratic and financial matters in a foreign language.

Sometimes a trial period will end with a change of heart, as Jim Grimshaw explained:

> *We came here for five months, hoping to find somewhere to buy. We thought it would be more cultural than Spain. But there is too much building here. We don't think we would be able to sell a house again later. So we are having another think.*

John Cunningham had intended to buy in Southern Cyprus: *'We had put down a deposit of C£2,000 but after 12 months nothing had happened on the site. Then we came north and now we've decided to buy here instead.'* Such changes of mind may result in disappointment and small financial loss but that must be preferable to making an expensive mistake that might be difficult to reverse.

LEARNING THE LANGUAGE

Neither Greek nor Turkish is amongst the world's most commonly spoken languages. Consequently most people who move to Cyprus are going to have to make a special effort to get to grips with the local language. It is unusual to meet an expat who can speak either of them fluently even after many years on the island.

According to some estimates, up to 15% of the vocabulary of both north and south Cyprus differs from that of mainland Greece and Turkey, and people intending to settle in **Southern Cyprus** need to be aware that the Greek Cypriot dialect is markedly different from the sort of Greek taught on most courses in Greece and the UK. Although traditionally very different, the Turkish spoken by most people in **Northern Cyprus** today is not so different from that spoken on mainland Turkey, as more and more mainland Turks take up residence there. Indeed, some people fear that there will soon be almost no-one left on the island speaking the old Turkish-Cypriot dialect.

The good news for intending retirees is that the majority of people in Southern Cyprus have some familiarity with English. Perhaps more surprisingly, the same is also true in Northern Cyprus; given that most work available is in tourism, many of the settlers from the mainland know some English, although in Lefkoşa it's harder to find English-speakers. Many people therefore decide that they need not make the effort to learn the local language. However, if you don't do so you will miss out on much of what makes local society tick. And if you make even the smallest effort to speak Greek or Turkish the locals will really appreciate it.

Learning Greek may be slightly easier than learning Turkish, if only because the sentence structure is similar to that of English and many words in the English language have their roots in ancient Greek. Most people, for example, would recognise the Greek words *'ego'* for 'I' and *'exodus'* for 'exit', were it not for the fact that they are concealed behind an unfamiliar alphabet; if you do nothing else, at least make sure you learn the Greek alphabet before moving to Southern Cyprus because not everything is transliterated.

Learning Turkish is complicated not just by an unfamiliar vocabulary derived in part from Arabic and Farsi but also by a sentence structure in which the verb appears at the end and takes different endings to indicate not just the tense but the person involved. The two comforts are that you pronounce every letter (with one exception) in Turkish just as it appears and that the language is logical with few irregular verbs.

Since learning either language is going to be testing and most people find it harder to learn a new language as they age, it is never a moment too soon to embark on Greek or Turkish lessons. However, it probably pays to be realistic about your chances of achieving fluency. As Gina Ghillyer pointed out: *'People round Pafos speak such a broad dialect. Even if I do say things in Greek they tend to laugh at me.'*

Good luck! Kali tikhi! Bol şans!

Tips for Learning Greek or Turkish

- **Enrol on a Greek or Turkish Course.** Local authorities and colleges of further education often offer evening classes aimed at people who want to obtain GCSEs or A levels. These classes usually follow the normal academic year, but you may also find shorter, more intensive 'holiday Greek' and 'holiday Turkish' classes on offer as well (they usually start in the spring).
- **Find a Private Tutor.** Private Greek and Turkish courses are likely to be more expensive (£15-£20 per hour) and more difficult to organise. Ultimately, however, they may prove more useful, especially once you get past being an absolute beginner since private tuition usually works best for improving conversational skills rather than for learning grammar (unless you land a tutor who is a properly trained teacher). To link up with a native speaker of Greek or Turkish who lives near you, you could try putting an advertisement in a local paper or making contact through an English-language school or an ethnic restaurant. Once in Cyprus look in the classified ads in the English-language press for people offering one-on-one tuition.

- **Buy a Self-Study Book and Cassette Package.** Self-study courses allow students to work at their own pace. The BBC (☎0870-2415 490; www.bbcshop.com) produces excellent workbooks and audio cassettes at various levels, while the book-cassette packages produced by the *Teach Yourself* series are also particularly good for both Greek and Turkish. *Linguaphone* (☎0800-282417; www.linguaphone.co.uk) distributes more elaborate (and more expensive) self-study courses.
- **Study on the Internet.** Studying Greek and Turkish on-line is becoming more popular although on its own it is likely to prove a slow way of learning and one that requires a lot of willpower. If you do want to try it look at www.cybc.com.cy/Learn.htm, which is hosted by the Cyprus Broadcasting Corporation, or try www.ilearngreek.com Online Turkish courses can be found at www.practicalturkish.com, www.learningpracticalturkish.com, www.turkish-center.com, www.turkishlanguage.co.uk and www.online-turkish.com.
- **Take a Study Holiday in Greece or Turkey.** In Cyprus itself organized language courses are few and far between although the University of Cyprus in Lefkosia does run intensive summer schools (☎22 43 47 90, smgreek@ucy.ac.cy). However, there is nothing to stop you heading back to source and looking for a Greek course in Athens or a Turkish course in İstanbul. So long as you bear in mind the dialect differences, such courses offer a fantastic way to make a start on the languages. Most involve total immersion and incorporate a programme of social, cultural and sporting activities to supplement academic study. Contact a UK-based language school such as www.languagesabroad.co.uk to find a suitable course.
- **Join a Greek, Turkish or Cypriot Society.** Find out if any Anglo-Greek, Anglo-Turkish or Anglo-Cypriot clubs or societies exist in your area as these will organise social events to soften the culture shock of life in Cyprus. Your local further education institute, university or library should be able to help you find an address.
- **Watch Greek or Turkish Television.** Although there is a lot of dross on Cypriot television, watching local sitcoms in particular can help you pick up the language, with the visual prompts helping you to understand what is going on.

- **Listen to Greek, Turkish or Cypriot Radio.** Listening to the radio is another wonderful way to immerse yourself in Greek and Turkish. Realistically, however, it will be years rather than months before most people can understand more than the gist of what is being said.
- **Read Greek, Turkish or Cypriot Newspapers and Books.** Reading something light, perhaps even an illustrated children's book in Greek or Turkish, will help your vocabulary enormously. Getting to grips with local newspapers can also help. Start with the headlines and lighter features and work up to the heavier political pages.

RESIDENCE REGULATIONS

Take a deep breath and hold it – most applications for licences, visas, permits etc require an inordinate amount of time and patience, especially in Northern Cyprus where the rules often change before the ink has dried on the paper announcing them. The good news is that both parts of Cyprus are fairly relaxed about regulations, although in Southern Cyprus you should expect a gradual tightening up as the country revises its procedures to fall into line with EU requirements.

Visa and Entry Requirements

EU citizens, Canadians, Australians, New Zealanders and Americans can visit **Northern and Southern Cyprus** for three months without a visa. However, if you have a stamp from Northern Cyprus in your passport it is still theoretically possible that you could be refused admission to Southern Cyprus and even to Greece; ask to have the stamp put on a separate piece of paper – the Northern Cypriot authorities are used to this request and have the requisite looseleaf slips readily to hand. In reality it is very unlikely that Greece would refuse to admit an EU citizen because of the fuss it would cause; the Southern Cypriots reserve the right to fine people who arrive from the north but so far they have not actually done this.

At the time of writing the following borders between north and south were open to EU citizens:

- Ledra Palace (Lefkoşa/Lefkosia: pedestrians only)
- Metehan/Kermia (Lefkoşa/Lefkosia: cars)
- Beyarmudu/Pyla (near the BSB at Dhekelia: cars)
- Akyar (nr Gazimağusa/Famagusta on the Paralimni-Mağusa road: cars)

Visa Extensions

It is usually quite easy to renew your visa in **Southern Cyprus**; you simply go to the Aliens Branch of the local police station and show proof that you have sufficient funds to support yourself.

To renew your visa in **Northern Cyprus** usually means an overnight trip to Turkey to avoid the bureaucracy of official extension. This is complicated by the relative shortage and cost of flights, although the new Pegasus flights from Lefkoşa to Adana in Turkey should help alleviate this problem. Of course there are always the ferries (see *Getting There and Away* below). However, these require a lot of queuing, delays and general aggravation. Now that the border to the south is open some expats have tried to argue that crossing the Attila Line constitutes 'leaving the country' for purposes of getting a new visa. According to June Hall: *'This is a hot topic among TRNC residents because there is a big fine if you fail to renew your visa.' However*, this is bending the spirit if not the letter of the law and you should not be surprised if the authorities refuse to accept this as adequate.

Residency

Acquiring residency in **Southern Cyprus** is not difficult although you will be expected to show proof that you can support yourself. Currently this is taken to mean that a couple has an annual income of C£12,000. You should take evidence of this to the Aliens Branch of the local police who will then process your application and issue your Alien's Residence Card (ARC) and residency permit ('pink slip') in return for C£5; if there is a delay they will give you receipts for your payments to show in the interim. However, as there is an EU directive that people resident in any EU country for more than five years should be eligible for residency rights it is likely that this system will soon change.

ID Cards: After you have been living in Southern Cyprus for six months you can apply for an identity card. You will need to get your ARC and residency permit first, then take them to the Immigration Department together with your passport and birth certificate. Don't expect it to be issued on the spot.

In order to buy a house in **Northern Cyprus** you need to be a resident there. You need to apply in writing to the Migration Officer of the Ministry of the Interior in Lefkoşa. Since the process for acquiring residency can take up to two years to complete, it probably pays to get a solicitor to help you. If you own a property in the north, getting residency is virtually automatic, so to square this seeming circle the process of organising residency is normally carried out alongside that of buying a property. Perhaps surprisingly you do not have to prove that you can support yourself although the police and Interpol will carry out a search to ensure that you have no criminal record. Once residency has been granted it does not have to be renewed every few years as it does on the Turkish mainland.

Retirement Status

If you want to retire to **Southern Cyprus** permanently you should apply to the Chief Immigration Officer for an Immigration Permit. You will need to fill out Form M67 and provide a short c.v. together with original documentary proof of a secure income (a pension, dividends, interest on savings etc) of at least C£5,600 a year. Your application will be considered by the Immigration Control Board who will refer their findings to the Minister of the Interior for approval.

Help is at Hand...

Bureaucracy was one of the biggest complaints amongst the retired expats interviewed for this book. So if you live in or around Pafos you may be interested to hear about Gwenny Thomas (☎9941 2925) whose name cropped up regularly in conversations. Gwenny will take on the time-consuming business of cutting through the red tape on your behalf. Of course she charges for her services. However, unless you are on your uppers your may think her fee a small price to pay for not having to stand in endless queues arguing with bureaucrats in clumsy Greek.

If you want to retire to **Northern Cyprus** permanently you need to apply in writing to the Migration Officer of the Ministry of the Interior in Lefkoşa. Do not expect a speedy reply.

Citizenship

If you have been resident in **Southern Cyprus** for seven years you can apply for citizenship. You will need to prove that you have been on the island for the entire year leading up to the application and will have to produce a birth certificate, a copy of your passport, a character reference, two photographs and a completed application form (M127). You will also need to advertise your request for citizenship in a Cypriot newspaper for two consecutive days.

A foreign resident married to a Southern Cypriot can apply for citizenship after two years of 'harmonious cohabitation'. In addition to the paperwork listed above you will need to show your marriage certificate, your spouse's passport and a certificate from the chairman (*muktar)* of the local communal council confirming that you have been living together for the two years preceding the application. You will need to be legally resident in Cyprus and will have to fill out Form M125 to apply for citizenship on these terms.

So long as **Northern Cyprus** goes unrecognised by the outside world no foreigner is likely to want – or be advised – to take up citizenship there. However, in theory you can apply for citizenship after five years' residence. There are rumours that this may be pushed up to 15 years in the near future although this flies in the face of EU advice.

Useful Contact

Immigration Dept (Ministry of the Interior): ☎2280 4510, www.moi.gov.cy/cc; 125 Athalassas Ave, Lefkosia.

Embassies and Consulates

Once resident in Cyprus, it is advisable to register with your embassy or consulate. This enables the authorities to keep you up to date with any information you need as a citizen resident overseas; in the event of an emergency, registration also helps the authorities to trace individuals. Your embassy or consulate can also help with information regarding your status overseas, advise on diplomatic or passport problems, and help in the case of an emergency (e.g. the death of a relative overseas). However, you should bear in mind that the British Embassy cannot bale you out if you break Cypriot laws. Nor will they loan you money except in the most extreme of circumstances.

Because **Northern Cyprus** is not recognised by any country other than Turkey it has 'foreign representation' rather than embassies. From your point of view this is a matter of semantics.

Cypriot Embassies and Consulates in the UK

Embassy of the Republic of Cyprus: 93 Park St, London W1Y 4ET; ☎020-7499 8272; fax 020-7491 0691.

Representation of the Turkish Republic of Northern Cyprus: 29 Bedford Square, London WC1B 3EG; ☎020-7631 1920; fax 020-7462 9785.

British Embassies and Consulates in Cyprus

British Embassy in the Republic of Cyprus: Alexandrou Palli St, CY-1587 Lefkosia; ☎357 22 86 11 00; fax 357 22 86 11 25, www.british.org.cy.

British Representation in the Turkish Republic of Northern Cyprus: Mehmet Akif Caddesi 29, Köşkluçiftlik, Lefkoşa; ☎227 4938.

For information on all aspects of residency and acquiring citizenship in **Southern Cyprus** contact the Immigration Department in Lefkosia (☎2280 4510; migration@crmd.moi.gov.cy). The government website, www.cyprus.gov.cy, is also very helpful. Less useful but still a starting point for enquiries is the website of the government of **Northern Cyprus** (www.trncgov.com).

GETTING THERE & AWAY

Scheduled Flights

Since there are so many options for flying to Cyprus you should always spend plenty of time doing your research before booking. Useful websites that search for the cheapest flights available at any time are www.whichbudget.com, www.skyscanner.net and www.openjet.com. It's also worth trying less obvious sales outlets such as Teletext since these too can throw up unexpected bargains.

Remember that high-season fares are usually charged from June through September, over Christmas and the New Year, and over Easter, with smaller price hikes sometimes applied over European half-term periods too.

The South

Several scheduled airlines fly to Pafos and Larnaca in **Southern Cyprus** although so far none of the low-cost fliers has taken the island on. However, since Stelios HajIoannou, the founder of easyJet, is himself of Cypriot origin, there must be hope that the orange airline will soon be gracing the Cypriot tarmac.

The Southern Cyprus airport tax is included in the price of all tickets.

The North

Northern Cyprus's pariah status means that Lefkoşa's Ercan airport is only accessible by air via İstanbul, adding miles, pounds and hours to the journey. However. as a reward to the North for supporting reunification of the island in the 2004 referendum, it is possible that the economic embargo may gradually be relaxed to allow international flights to land; Azerbaijan Airlines is expected to be first to start flying to Ercan. The Northern Cyprus Tourism Centre (☎0207-631 1930; www.go-northcyprus.com) should have the latest information.

In 2006 easyJet started flights to İstanbul. It is possible that Pegasus will link its routes to theirs so that people can connect from İstanbul to Ercan, thereby reducing the fare. However, EU citizens can now cross the border to the south and use flights into and out of the Republic of Cyprus.

The Airlines

Airline services change frequently so it is best to check current routes on the internet and keep an eye on the travel press for the latest information.

British Airways: ☎0845-7733377; www.ba.com. Destinations: Larnaka, Pafos.

Cyprus Airways: ☎08000-0008; www.cyprusairways.com. Destinations: Larnaka, Pafos, Amman, Amsterdam, Athens, Bahrain, Beirut, Birmingham, Brussels, Cairo, Corfu, Damascus, Dubai, Frankfurt, Heraklion, Jeddah, London (Heathrow), London (Stansted), Manchester, Milan, Moscow, Paris, Riyadh, Rome, Tel Aviv, Thessaloniki, Vienna, Warsaw, Zurich.

Cyprus Turkish Airlines: ☎020-7930 4851, www.kthy.net. Destination: Ercan.

Egyptair: ☎0357-2255 9000. Destinations: Larnaka, Cairo.

El-Al Israeli Airlines: ☎0357-2557 4180. Destinations: Larnaka, Tel Aviv.

Emirates: ☎0357-2281 7616. Destinations: Larnaka, Dubai.

Eurocypria: ☎0357-2465 8000. Destinations: Larnaka, Rhodes, Heraklion.

Gulf Air: ☎0357-2237 4064. Destinations: Larnaka, Bahrain.

Kıbrıs Türk Hava Yolları (Cyprus Turkish Airlines): ☎020-7930 4851; from London: ☎228 3901; www.kthy.net. Twice-weekly flights from London to Lefkoşa via İzmir.

KLM: ☎0357-2267 1616. Destinations: Larnaka, Amsterdam.

Lufthansa: ☎0357-2287 3330, www.lufthansa.de. Destinations: Larnaka, Frankfurt.

Middle East Airlines: ☎0357-2267 0444. Destinations: Larnaka, Beirut.

Olympic Airways: ☎0357-2271 6500. Destinations: Larnaka, Athens.

Pegasus: ☎03-444 0737; www.flypgs.com. Destinations: Lefkoşa, Adana, Ankara, İstanbul

Royal Jordanian Airlines: ☎0357-2246 0295. Destinations: Larnaka, Amman.

Syrian Arab Airlines: ☎0357-2244 7100. Destinations: Larnaka, Damascus.

Tarom – Romanian Airlines: ☎0357-2237 4757. Destinations: Larnaka, Bucharest.

Turkish Airlines (THY): ☎020-7766 9300; www.thy.com. Flights from Heathrow and Manchester to Lefkoşa via İstanbul.

Charter Flights

These days there are few differences between charter and scheduled flights. However, scheduled flights usually operate all year round while many charter services tail off or vanish altogether in winter. Usually they are only available for fixed periods (e.g. 7 or 14 days) whereas you can buy scheduled flights for however long or short a time you want.

Websites selling flights

www.airflights.co.uk
www.avro.co.uk
www.cheapflights.com
www.lastminute.com
www.opodo.co.uk
www.statravel.co.uk
www.thomsonfly.com
www.firstchoice.co.uk
www.flightline.co.uk
www.flythomascook.com
www.dialaflight.com
www.excelairways.com
www.expedia.co.uk

Charters can be booked directly through the websites listed above; some can also be booked through travel agents. In 2006 Libra Holidays announced that it would be launching a new charter airline, ajet (www.ajet.com), to fly to Cyprus. However, at the time of writing it was still awaiting approval from the aviation authorities. Also at the time of writing Helios Airways was grounded pending the findings of an enquiry into a fatal air crash that took place in Greece in 2005.

Airports

Southern Cyprus has two international airports: Larnaka and Pafos. Larnaka airport (☎7777 8833) is 5km/3m east of Larnaka town while Pafos airport (☎7777 8833) is 15km/9m east of Pafos town.

Northern Cyprus has just the one airport, Ercan International (☎231 7340), which is 20km/13m south-east of Lefkoşa

Ferries

The South. Salamis Lines (☎2589 9999) has a twice-weekly summer-only ferry service from Piraeus in Greece to Lemesos. It departs Piraeus on Monday and Thursday at 8 pm.

Poseidon Lines and Salamis Lines used to connect Southern Cyprus with Greece and Haifa in Israel or Port Said in Egypt by boat on a weekly basis. However, the troubles in the Middle East mean that both services are currently mothballed and unlikely to restart any day soon.

The North. Frequent car ferries and catamarans link southern Turkey (Taşucu, Mersin, Alanya) with Northern Cyprus (Girne). The journey by catamaran generally takes two to three hours, that by car ferry around four hours. However, in winter the catamarans cannot always sail and the ferry crossing can triple in length while the captain waits for suitable sailing weather.

Ferries from Turkey to Cyprus

Akfer Denizcilik: ☎0324-741 4033; Taşucu İskelesi, Turkey. Daily high-speed catamarans. Car ferries most nights.

Akfer Denizcilik: ☎0242-512 8889; İskele Caddesi 86, Alanya, Turkey. Summer-only ferry services.

Akfer Denizcilik: ☎0392-815 6002; Girne, North Cyprus. Daily high-speed catamarans. Car ferries most nights.

Kıbrıs Denizcilik: ☎0324-233 9858; Mersin İskele, Turkey. Three times weekly car ferries from Mersin to Gazimağusa and vice versa. Large ships are more reliable in winter than the ferries/ catamarans from Taşucu and Alanya.

PREPARATIONS FOR DEPARTURE

If you are planning to move to Cyprus permanently you will need to begin preparations several months in advance. Every aspect of your daily life will need to be considered as you decide what should be cancelled in the UK, what transferred to Cyprus and how this should be done. For such an important undertaking a checklist is virtually essential. How your own list pans out will depend on your personal requirements but the items below are likely to appear on everyone's.

Banking

Whether you intend to live in Cyprus permanently or simply spend a lot of time there, you will probably need to open a local bank account.

If you are spending a trial period there or visiting to look at properties you can withdraw money from your UK bank account from a Cypriot ATM on either side of the Attila Line. However, the charges mean that this can quickly become expensive; nor will the exchange rate always work in your favour. Many people wait until they have moved to Cyprus before opening an account but estate agents often advise you to open an account while you are looking for a property because it could help smooth and speed up the sale.

To open an account before you leave the UK you need to visit either the London office of a Cypriot bank or a British bank such as HSBC that is represented in Cyprus; setting up an account should be a matter of completing a few forms provided that you can prove your identity sufficiently to satisfy the bank manager. Although some people feel more confident about opening an account with the Cypriot branch of a UK bank, they will find that these operate in exactly the same way as the Cypriot national banks and are completely separate from their UK parent companies.

Banks in Southern Cyprus

Alpha Bank Ltd: www.alphabank.com.

Arab Bank plc: www.arabbank.com.

Bank of Cyprus Ltd: www.bankofcyprus.com.

Commercial Bank of Greece (Cyprus) Ltd

Cyprus Popular (Laiki) Bank Ltd: (www.cypruspopular.bank.com).

Hellenic Bank Ltd: (www.hellenicbank.com).

Banks in Northern Cyprus

Garanti Bankası: www.garantibank.com

HSBC: ☎0392-815 9988; fax 0392-815 9980; Ziya Rızkı Caddesi 16, Girne.

HSBC: ☎357 22 376116; fax 357 22 37612; Dositheou 7, Block C, 1071 Lefkosia.

İktisat Bank: ☎228 5300, Girne

Kıbrıs Vakıf Bankası: ☎815 1757, Girne; 228 3212, Lefkoşa; ☎366 4990, Mağusa

Oyak Bankası: www.oyakbank.com.tr

T.C. Ziraat Bankası: www.ziraat.com.tr

Türkiye İş Bankası: www.isbank.com.tr

HSBC is the only British bank that operates in both **North and South Cyprus** and is probably the best bet for transferring money from abroad, especially in the north. In **Southern Cyprus** the following banks should also be used to dealing with cash transfers from abroad: Alpha Bank, Bank of Cyprus, Co-operative Central Bank, Cyprus Popular (Laiki) Bank, Hellenic Bank and Universal Savings Bank. In **Northern Cyprus** try Garanti Bankası or Türkiye İş Bankası since they are branches of two of the largest banks in Turkey. HSBC has English-speaking staff but people interviewed for this book reported that they still had to jump through a lot of hoops before they could open an account there.

For details of banking once you are settled in Cyprus see Chapter 8: *Personal Finance*.

Medical Matters

An essential part of your preparations should be a visit to your GP to have a final check-up before moving abroad. During this visit you can explain your plans to the doctor and get a quick summary of your medical history together with information on the generic names of any regularly used prescription medicines. You should expect to pay £10 for a straightforward copy of your medical records and considerably more if parts have to be obtained from a hospital or other medical facility. You can write to your doctor to ask for a copy of your records; if you do this it is suggested that you send the letter by recorded delivery; legally you are entitled to a reply within 40 days.

You should also visit your dentist and optician as you may feel more confident getting your teeth and eyes checked in the UK with a familiar dentist and optician. Take any prescription for glasses with you to have it made up in Cyprus where prices are lower than in the UK.

If you are already receiving a state pension you should also obtain Form E121 from The Pension Service section of the UK Department for Work and Pensions (see below). You give this to the Southern Cypriot health authorities to gain access to their healthcare system. If you are retiring to Cyprus before reaching pensionable age and don't intend to work there it may still be possible to receive free healthcare for a limited period by applying to the DWP for Form E106. However, not everyone is eligible for this.

Further details on all the above topics are available in the DWP Leaflet SA29 – *Going Abroad and Social Security Benefits* – which can be downloaded from their website. Further information on medical matters, including on the European health Insurance Card (EHIC) which provides for reciprocal medical care within other EU countries for up to three months at a time, can be found in Chapter 9: *Healthcare.*

DWP Contact Details

Department for Work & Pensions: The Pension Service, International Pension Centre, Medical Benefits Section, Tyneview Park, Whitely Road, Newcastle-upon-Tyne NE98 1BA; ☎0191 218 7777; www.dwp.gov.uk.

Mail Forwarding

Whether you have sold your UK property, are letting it out or simply leaving it vacant you will need your post forwarded to your new address in Cyprus. Of course if you are keeping your UK address, you are likely to receive more post than if you leave the UK completely.

If you have a trusted neighbour or your tenants are friends ask them to check your post, throw away obvious junk mail and readdress important-looking mail to you. Alternatively you can arrange to have your post officially redirected by the Royal Mail by filling out a form at the post office. Mail can only be redirected for two years and the service costs from £13.90 (one month) to £69.80 (one year) per surname. Special Delivery and mail that requires a signature cannot be forwarded. The service works efficiently although inevitably your post takes longer to arrive, something to bear in mind if you are waiting for anything important or time-limited such as a tax form. To organise mail redirection from Cyprus ☎0044-1752-387116.

Otherwise commercial mail-forwarding services can be found by putting 'accommodation address' into a Google search or by asking at your nearest business centre. Such services allow you to use their address and have your mail forwarded once a week for around £15 per month. Some people maintain an accommodation address permanently to ensure receipt of such vital documents as reminders to renew their UK photocard driving licence.

Poste Restante. In the short-term you may need to rely on the poste restante services offered by most main post offices. When you want to pick your mail up, go to the relevant post office with your passport or another form of identification. Some post offices return mail that has been awaiting collection for what they judge to be too long a time.

In **Southern Cyprus** the following post offices have poste restante facilities: Lefkosia (☎2230 3219; Plateia Eleftherias), Lemesos (☎2580 2259; Gladstonos 3); Larnaka (☎2480 2406, Plateia Vasileos Pavlou); and Pafos (☎2694 0220; Nikidimou Mylona).

In **Northern Cyprus** the main post offices in Girne, Mağusa and Lefkoşa also offer poste restante services; in practise once you get to know your local postman they will probably hold onto your mail for you anyway.

Pensions

You may want to arrange for state and/or occupational pensions to be paid into your new Cypriot bank account. To do this you should contact the UK pension service (www.thepensionservice.gov.uk; ☎ 0845-606060) and ask for details of overseas direct payment in local currency. For occupational and private pensions contact the individual providers who will advise you on what to do.

If you move to Cyprus before reaching retirement age and don't intend to work there you should arrange to continue paying national insurance contributions in the UK in order to qualify for a British state pension when you reach 65. Before you go, seek advice on this issue from the HM Revenue and Customs National Insurance Contributions Office (☎0845 302 1479; www.hmrc.gov.uk/nic/).

For more details see Pensions and Exportable UK Benefits in Chapter 8: *Personal Finance.*

Pets

The South. Cats and dogs can be brought into Southern Cyprus under the EU Pet Travel Scheme (PETS) which was designed to simplify travelling with pets inside the area of the European Union. However, it can still be a lengthy and expensive (around £200) process since you must first obtain an EU pet passport. This means that your pet must be micro-chipped and given a rabies vaccination at least 21 days before you plan to travel. This procedure must be carried out by a government-authorised vet. Immediately before you fly (i.e. no sooner than 48 hours beforehand) a vet must also certify that the animal has been given flea, tick and worm treatment.

When you arrive in Southern Cyprus with your cat or dog you will have to show all the appropriate paperwork to a Veterinary Officer or to Customs Officers acting on behalf of the Veterinary Services; you need to give 48 hours' advance notice of the animal's arrival to ensure that someone is available to carry out the inspection. If all the papers are in order you will have to pay around C£65 in handling charges but will be free to take your pet home with you. If, however, something is wrong with the paperwork your cat or dog could end up quarantined for up to six months at your expense, so don't take any risks. If you do not get the required anti-parasite treatment mentioned above you will have to pay C£26 for it at the airport and your pet will have to undergo one month's quarantine.

No American pit bull terriers, Japanese tosas, or Argentinian or Brazilian mastiffs may be brought into the country, even if they have been microchipped and vaccinated.

> Whether you choose to live in the north or south you need to be aware that local attitudes towards dogs and cats rarely coincide with those in the UK. Having animals neutered is very unusual which means there are always abandoned puppies and kittens looking for homes. Harder to deal with is the fact that some pet animals end up poisoned or shot, something you need to think about before bringing yours from the UK.

Some but not all ferry companies and airlines will carry accompanied pets; see the DEFRA website for details. If you are flying BA (☎0870-850 9850) they will charge around £4 per kilo of the weight of the animal and its container plus a handling charge of at least £20. You will have to be on the same flight as your pet which will fly as excess baggage. Its container must be made of plastic or wood and must be big enough for it to stand, turn and lie down. You must not sedate or feed the animal before the flight; nor can its container have anything inside it other than a blanket and a non-spillable water container.

PETS is supervised by DEFRA (the Department for the Environment, Food and Rural Affairs, www.defra.gov.uk) which keeps the most up-to-date information on conditions. Further information is available from the nearest Cypriot consulate or the PETS helpline (☎0870-241 1710).

The North. Animals imported into Northern Cyprus also need a certificate of good health issued by a Western vet but will have to be quarantined in kennels in Lefkoşa for two weeks. If you take your pet from Southern Cyprus to Northern Cyprus this could compromise its right to return to the UK without having to go into quarantine.

Useful Contacts

Airpets Oceanic: ☎01753-685571; www.airpets.com. Pet exports, pet travel schemes, boarding, transportation by road/air to and from all UK destinations.

Department of Veterinary Services: 1417 Lefkosia; ☎0357-22 80 52 35; fax 0357-22 80 51 74; animal.health@vs.moa.gov.cy

Ammochostos District Veterinary Office: ☎2472 1571; Ormidia.

Larnaka District Veterinary Office: ☎2430 4275

Lefkosia District Veterinary Office: ☎2280 5240

Lemesos District Veterinary Office: ☎2581 9512

Pafos District Veterinary Office: ☎2630 6269

Pet Plan: ☎0800-107 0204; www.petplan.co.uk. Travel insurance for pets.

Removals

When considering what to take with you you should start with what you think is a list of essentials and then prune it down. Only take what is absolutely irreplaceable and remember that heavy items will inevitably bump up shipping costs.

The approximate charge for transporting your belongings from the UK to Cyprus is £120 to £150 per cubic metre plus a fixed fee for administration and paperwork. Typically you should expect the total cost to come to around £2,500-£4,000. The whole process normally takes at least three weeks.

Despite the trade embargo most international removals firms will also move your belongings to **Northern Cyprus.** If you have any trouble, try contacting Olaytrans Ltd (☎0090-392 366 6540) or Armen Shipping (☎0090-392 366 4086).

For information on importing a car into Cyprus, see Cars & Motoring in Chapter 7: *Quality of Life.*

Whatever you choose to bring to the island will arrive at the port of Lemesos (in the south) or Gazimağusa (in the north) and then be trucked to your home.

> Although there are numerous removal firms, which advertise in Cypriot property magazines look for those which are members of the British Association of Removers (www.removers.org.uk; ☎01923-699480) as these are likely to be the most reputable companies. BAR has set up an International Movers Mutual Insurance to compensate clients of any of its member companies in the event of loss or damage to cargo; in the case of a member's bankruptcy the removal will be completed by another BAR member.
>
> Before you start phoning for quotes, note that there is a useful website which does the bulk of the work for you: www.reallymoving.com. Simply type in the pick-up and drop-off points and a rough estimate of how many cubic feet you'll be moving (their estimator will work this out for you) and your request will be e-mailed to several shipping companies. Over the following few days personalised quotes should start trickling into your inbox.

Removals Checklist

- If you are moving to either part of Cyprus permanently you can import all your furniture and household effects from the UK either duty-free or for a negligible sum.
- Before moving you should compile an inventory of all the goods to be transported. This list should be presented to the Cypriot Consulate together with a completed customs clearance form; the inventory will then be stamped for a small fee. The removals company should handle most of the paperwork for you.
- Furniture and other large items from an English home may not be

suitable for a beachfront villa. It may be more sensible to sell most of your furniture and white goods, and buy new things once you arrive in Cyprus.

- Electrical items cost about the same in Cyprus as in the UK. You may be tempted to bring yours from home but remember that finding suitable spare parts may be tricky. Unless you have just invested in a top-of-the-range fridge-freezer it is probably best to leave your old electrical items at home and buy new ones on the island.
- If you want to move something unusual such as a vintage car or a horse, try Brookfields Removals (www.brookfields-removals.co.uk). They can come up with a quote for moving nearly anything.

Removals Companies

Dolphin Movers: ☎020 8804 7700; www.dolphinmovers.com; 2 Haslemere Business Centre, Lincoln Way, Enfield EN1 1TE.

Fred Olsen Agencies Ltd: ☎01473-292480; www.fredolsen.co.uk; Fred Olsen House, White House Rd, Ipswich IP1 5LL.

MK Nejati & Sons Ltd: ☎0392-366 9979; nejati@cc.emu.edu.tr; Nejati House, 5 Hükümet Caddesi, Mağusa.

Pickfords: www.pickfords.com.

Customs

The South. Now that Southern Cyprus has entered the EU you can import whatever you want so long as it is for personal use rather than for resale. Customs officers have a list of quantities to use as guidelines in deciding whether you are abusing the system; so, for example, 10 litres of spirits, 90 litres of wine and 800 cigarettes are regarded as being for 'personal use'; anything more would be assumed to be for resale.

It is permissible to take advantage of differing rates of VAT within the EU countries to import some items for less than they cost in Cyprus (and vice versa). However, Cyprus' accession to the EU means that there are no longer duty-free facilities for EU citizens at the ports and airports.

Note that you are not allowed to import fruit, vegetables, seeds, bulbs or cuttings into Southern Cyprus without written permission from the Ministry of Agriculture and Natural Resources. Since this is intended to protect Cypriot farming from contamination you should not attempt to get round this rule, however much you love that special rose-bush. Not surprisingly you are also forbidden to import guns, ammunition, flick knives, daggers and swords, pornography, counterfeit goods, uncooked meat and fish, animals and birds (for the importation of pets see that section above).

You can import all your **household furnishings** duty-free, apart from a fee of C£4 per electrical item, under the EU's Transfer of Normal Place of Residence Regulations. For information about importing your car see Cars and Motoring in Chapter 6: *Adapting to Your New Life*.

There is no problem with importing most **prescription drugs** provided you bring only what would be regarded as enough for personal use. However, if you need to import any narcotics (i.e. morphine) or pyschotropics (i.e. diazepam) you will need a declaration of authorisation from the UK medical authorities dated no later than 30 days before you arrive in Cyprus. If you need more information contact the Department of Pharmaceutical Services in Lefkosia (☎2240 7110).

The North. You are also allowed to import your personal effects into Northern Cyprus free of charge, as well as being able to bring in the usual 400 cigarettes, 150cc of alcohol and 150cc of wine free of charge. Jeremy Hall is keen on gardening and DIY so he imported a rotivator, welding set and air compressor through Girne. '*The Customs guys were happy with everything else but not with these. Maybe they thought I was going to sell them? Or they were just unsure what they were for.*' He also brought a computer over from the UK in his own car and had no trouble importing it duty-free.

Exchange Control. You can import as much cash as you want into **Southern Cyprus**. However, you must declare the import or export of any amount in excess of C£7,300/€12,500 or the equivalent in any other currency.

You can import and export up to the equivalent of US$10,000 into **Northern Cyprus.** Bear in mind that the Turkish lira is rarely wanted anywhere other than in Turkey and Northern Cyprus.

Useful Contact

Customs & Excise Department: ☎357 22 60 17 22, www.mof.gov.cy/ce; Corner of Mich. Karaoli & Gr. Afxentiou, Lefkosia.

Tying Up Loose Ends Checklist

- Dispose of anything you don't want to take with you via ebay, a car boot sale or charity shops.
- Arrange disconnection of gas, electricity, water and phone. At same time cancel contracts with all utility companies and arrange to settle outstanding bills. If you are renting out your house take meter readings for gas and electricity and settle own bills before tenants move in.
- Decide whether to take your car with you or sell it and buy a new one (see Chapter 6: *Adapting to Your New Life*).
- Notify the bank, credit-card company, DVLC and passport office of your new address.
- Notify doctor, dentist, optician and vet of your plans
- Cancel gym, book and wine club memberships. Cancel subscriptions to newspapers and magazines or arrange to have them redirected.
- If you are renting out your house make inventory of items left in house to attach to tenancy agreement.
- Return library books.
- Stop milk and newspapers.

Part two

A New Home in Cyprus

Where to Retire

CHAPTER SUMMARY

- You will need to decide **whether to settle in Northern or Southern Cyprus** and then whether you want to live in a **coastal resort,** an **inland village** or in **Lefkosia/Lefkoşa**.
- Some people like to live close to **other expats**; others will want to head for the hills to escape them.
- It is important to try and foresee **future developments**, especially further building work that could affect your own property.
- In **Southern Cyprus** most British retirees have settled in and around Pafos. There are smaller communities in Lemesos, Larnaka, Ayia Napa, Polis, Paralimni and in many of the Troodos villages. Very few foreigners have settled in Lefkosia.
- In **Northern Cyprus** most British retirees have settled in around Girne although there are also small expat communities in Mağusa and Lefke. Few foreigners have settled in Lefkoşa.

CHOOSING THE RIGHT LOCATION FOR RETIREMENT

There is nothing more important than picking the right place to spend your retirement. Cyprus may be small but it is still fairly diverse and each area has its own attractions. In particular you need to make that crucial decision as to whether to settle north or south of the Attila Line.

Many expats spend long hours researching the areas that interest them in libraries and on the internet. Others buy on gut instinct having fallen in love with a specific area. However, the best advice is to spend as much time as possible on the island during the different seasons so that you can evaluate what each area to offer for yourself.

It is important to sort out your priorities early on. Are you a full-on city-dweller who needs the liveliness of a decent-sized town and a range of shops and cultural amenities? Or are you a country-lover who is seeking tranquillity and solitude? Do you crave healthy salt air and the holiday atmosphere of the coast, or are the rugged mountains of the interior more your thing? Be warned that friends and family can sometimes try and put you off altogether or try and persuade you to stick with the familiar when what you really want is a change. As long as you are confident that you have done the legwork you should hold onto what you think is right for you regardless.

Coastal Resort, Inland Village or Capital City?

The majority of people head straight for the coast. Being able to live near the sea is something many people dream about people, especially after wonderful, sun-soaked summer holidays spent lounging on Cypriot sand. And why not? After all, during the hot summer months sea breezes make the intense heat more bearable and many people love the idea of being able to swim in the warm waters of the Med. However, the dream has its downside which is that the tourist hordes have exactly the same idea, invading in high season and taking over those once quiet beaches, packing the roads with their hired cars and partying loudly into the early hours.

Unfortunately since everyone tends to have the same idea, properties close to a beach and with a sea view are always the most desirable and hence most expensive. You may also find that you are not allowed to build as close to the sea as you would like – in Northern Cyprus, for example, you are not normally allowed to build closer than 100m to the sea and in Southern Cyprus no closer than 90m to the sea.

In any case not everyone wants to live in a seaside resort all year round. Much of inland Cyprus is still relatively unspoilt and plots of land are often much cheaper there than on the coast. The infrastructure may be less developed but there will be more of a sense of community. For some people that sense of community combined with the greater peace and serenity will more than make up for the drive down to the beach.

A few people will also feel happy living in Lefkosia because it has so much more to offer in terms of cultural amenities and shops.

Living With Locals or Compatriots?

You may have imagined that by moving to Cyprus you would be escaping the rat race to live a bucolic life amid the locals as described by British retiree Sheila Hawkins in her popular trilogy of books about life on the Akamas Peninsula in the 1980s and 90s. However, the reality is that the sheer volume of foreigners who already own property in Cyprus means that you are rarely likely to find yourself living far away from someone else from the UK. Even houses in the mountain villages are increasingly being snapped up by foreigners. Although they may be more authentically Cypriot than the coastal resorts and the foreigners who live in them may have moved there for precisely that reason, don't fool yourself that you will be able to find a culturally intact mountain village where you can live in splendid isolation – those days are long gone.

Along the coast, it is impossible to live in a purely Cypriot community any more; and in areas such as Pafos and Ayia Napa the British live in virtual expat ghettoes. In such settlements the only native Cypriot face you are likely to see will be that of the gardener – and even that is less and less likely since many menial jobs are carried out by immigrants from Sri Lanka and the Middle East.

However, it is not always a bad thing to be living close to other expatriates. In such areas the British often set up their own social clubs offering all sorts of leisure activities which make it easier to settle in and find new friends. Many expats also find the presence of their fellow countrymen a positive plus when it comes to easing themselves into the local culture.

What Changes Are Likely to Occur?

Cyprus is going through a period of rapid development and no matter where you buy, the area is unlikely to remain as you found it. It is wise to be realistic about the likelihood of change, especially when it comes to the possibility of new buildings going up in the vicinity of your des res that could rob you, for example, of your treasured sea view.

Cypriot developers constantly look for new areas that are not already over-run with expats and where prices are still attractive to the international community. At the time of writing, for example, it was clear that some of them were keen to push as far into the unspoilt Karpaz Peninsula as possible.

If you are buying off-plan, be sure to ask about likely future developments which might turn a bijou set of apartments into an ugly housing estate. However, as Heather O'Neill pointed out:

Even if the developer tells you their own plans, that doesn't mean another company won't have projects that will affect you. You can go to the UK for three months and come back to find a new building going up right in front of you.

Other Considerations

Ease of Access. Despite Cyprus's small size it's still worth considering the proximity of the nearest airport, not least because the closer it is, the more likely it is that friends and family will visit. Cyprus has a poor public transport network – to take full advantage of everything the island has to offer you will either have to invest in a car or rent one on a regular basis.

Local Government. You may find that local services are very efficient and that planning and building regulations are dealt with quickly and efficiently. On the other hand things may be badly run and disproportionately expensive to remedy. Good places to find out this sort of information are the English-language magazines and newspapers, as well as other expat property owners.

Planning for the Future. The British Consulate advises people to think well ahead when considering where to buy their retirement home. It may be wonderful to live in a beautiful but remote spot in your fifties and early sixties, but as you get older the long trek to the nearest shops can become a burden, especially in winter. You should also consider the provision of medical facilities in the area where you are hoping to buy. Remember, too, that much new building on Cyprus consists of large villas. In the UK you can easily downsize to a flat or bungalow if you start to find stairs wearing or housework irksome. Here it may not be so easy.

Water Shortages. Constant sunshine may be great for sunbathers but can be dire for normal life in summer when water shortages sometimes persist for days at a time. Talk to other foreigners who have lived in the area for some time to find out how often this is a problem – estate agents are likely to downplay its significance.

Seasonal Population Fluctuations. If your property is part of a development where neighbouring units are let to holidaymakers you may want to consider the risk of constant partying during the high season. Conversely you need to be sure that the area won't become a ghost town in winter. Of course that wouldn't bother some people, as June Griffith explained: '*My sister's house is in a development of 23 properties and hers is the only one occupied all year. But she doesn't mind – she likes the peace and quiet.*' The only way to be completely sure what you are letting yourself in for is to visit in both high and low season – or rent for a while (see Chapter 2: *Basics*).

Overdevelopment. Since the majority people who move to the island are looking for properties near the sea, most of the coast of Southern Cyprus has already been heavily developed for tourism or second homes. Until recently Northern Cyprus had not been so comprehensively developed. However, that situation is changing fast and some expats worry that so much poorly-planned development is taking place that the north will soon be virtually indistinguishable from the south except in terms of prices.

THE MOST POPULAR AREAS FOR RETIREMENT

In **Southern Cyprus** most foreigners have settled in and around the big package-holiday resorts of Pafos, Larnaka, Lemesos and Ayia Napa. In particular British expatriates live in and round Pafos, a more appealing small town than Lemesos or Larnaka, both of which can sometimes feel shabby and run-down. Relatively few people have moved to Lefkosia even though there are some potentially very desirable residential districts there.

In **Northern Cyprus** almost all the foreigners who have settled have made homes in and around Girne and the foothills of the Kyrenia Mountains. Only recently have they started to discover Mağusa, even though it is an attractive town with a burgeoning café culture. In the last couple of years the coast immediately north of Mağusa as far as Boğaz has become increasingly popular. Until now few people have opted for Lefkoşa which is hardly surprising given its sleepy atmosphere. However, as in Lefkosia, Lefkoşa has some very attractive residential areas full of crumbling old houses that would make delightful homes were the political situation ever to encourage it.

Most people settling in Cyprus are buying new-build properties rather than existing houses or flats. In many cases they are buying off-plan before the property is even completed, relying on an architect's plans and drawings to show them what their home will look like. Inevitably there is scope for things to go wrong, and anyone buying something that is not yet complete should do their utmost to inspect other properties built by the same contractors to ensure that their workmanship is up to scratch.

SOUTHERN CYPRUS

Pafos (Paphos)

Population: approx 50,000.
Airport: Pafos International.

The most westerly of the towns on the south coast of Cyprus, Pafos has become more popular both with tourists and settlers since the opening of Pafos airport made it more readily accessible; an estimated 60% of the Brits based in Cyprus live in or around Pafos. It is a town that comes in two parts: **Ktima,** which is the older part at the top of a hill, and **Kato Pafos**, a more ramshackle settlement of hotels and restaurants ringing the harbour and castle and opening out into an archaeological site where impressive mosaics were discovered. Ktima mostly consists of a narrow shopping street ending at a covered market which sells a bit of fruit and veg and lots of tourist knick-knacks. There are some attractive old houses in this part of town but most Brits have opted for newly-built villas and apartments in Kato Pafos and adjacent areas. The two sections of Pafos were once quite separate. Nowadays modern development has joined up all the gaps and both parts are rapidly vanishing anyway amid the general development of the surrounding land either for tourism or, increasingly, for retirement homes.

According to some estimates more than 30,000 British people now have homes in and around Pafos. There are also many Eastern European residents, as well as assorted Russians, Syrians etc., which means that there are not as many Greek Cypriots in evidence as the population figure might initially suggest. All that makes for a situation in which it is easy to find other expats to socialise with and where anything that someone from Britain wants to buy is likely to be available, albeit at a mark-up on the UK price. In particular Pafos has a large population of foreign women living alone, either because their husbands are working in the Middle East or because they are widowed or divorced.

At the time of writing there were plans to move Pafos's fishing port to make space for a larger marina which will be ringed with restaurants, shops and upmarket accommodation. Work was also slated to begin on **Neapolis**, a vast new complex near Pafos which will incorporate a university, a state-of-the-art hospital and sheltered accommodation for the elderly.

West of Pafos, Brits have settled in large numbers at **Coral Bay** which has a good, if over-developed, beach, and in **Peyia** and **Geroskipou,** which are now little more than suburbs of Pafos. Property in and around Pafos tends to be slightly more expensive than elsewhere on the island.

Even further west is the **Akamas Peninsula**, the wildest part of southern Cyprus where development has been kept to a minimum so far but where the Laona Project has encouraged people to convert old stone properties into sustainable tourist accommodation.

RETIREMENT HOTSPOTS

Kamares is a newly-created 'village' near Pafos. Since it has been in existence for more than 10 years it feels more like a real village than some of the newer complexes. Many of the houses have terracotta pots set into their stone walls, and plants and trees have had time to get established so that they look less stark than in many other local developments. Three-bed villas with pools go for around C£200,000, although there are also some much pricier properties here.

Aphrodite Hills is a 'resort lifestyle development' midway between Pafos and Lemesos that started life in 1999. The first apartments were completed in 2003 and since then an 18-hole golf course, tennis academy, spa (The Retreat; www.aphroditehillsspa.com), shops, restaurants and five-star hotel have been added to the complex which boasts a 'village square' with a replica Byzantine chapel. A development company installed the infrastructure and now sells off-plan villas and apartments as well as plots of land to intending builders who normally have to start work on their plot within four years of buying it. So far 65% of buyers have been British. Since some people have bought more than one plot of land it is thought that there will be around 250 private homes on the site when it is completed. A one-bedroomed apartment cost C£200,000 and a two-bedroomed villa C£525,000 at the time of writing.

Lemesos (Limassol)

Population: approx.150,000.
Airports: Larnaka; Pafos.

As the Republic of Cyprus's second biggest town, Lemesos is a long-established settlement that lives for something more than tourism (i.e. wine-making, citrus production and port activity). The seafront has been pleasingly refurbished with a promenade and sculpture park and there has been some upgrading of the old town centre around the medieval castle where there are some fine, if crumbling, old Ottoman Greek buildings and lots of cafes and restaurants, some of them in converted carob warehouses. However, the town is hardly beautiful and the shops would not set most people's pulses racing.

Given the proximity of the Akrotiri Sovreign Base, Lemesos has had long experience with the British, especially with their squaddies. But since the fall of the Soviet Union, it has also become a popular playground for Russian businessmen and the inevitable prostitutes who seem to trail after them, which means that it has some decidedly sleazy nightlife.

Lemesos port is the largest on the island and is used by cruise ships as well as container vessels. The St Raphael Marina (☎2563 5800, www.raphael.com.cy) is also slated for expansion. Plans for a new Technological University of Cyprus in Lemesos mean that there is likely to be a rise in demand for rental accommodation for students. The University itself is to be housed in existing buildings such as the old post office that will be restored and converted.

Most package tourism to Lemesos is focused on the beaches to the east of town and this, too, is where some of the property development has taken place, especially around **Governor's Beach**, a whole 30km out of town. **Pervolia,** to the north-east, has become very popular with the British. However, there are some much more attractive old villages in the foothills of the Troodos to the north, amongst them **Dhora** and **Mousere**, where crumbling stone houses cry out for restoration. Even more picturesque, and already discovered by settlers, is the village of **Lofou,** a handy 18-kilometre drive out of Lemesos. Similarly appealing is **Lania**, where as many as 25% of the residents may now be expats.

Heading east towards Larnaka, there are some properties for sale in **Kellaki.** However, this is not as attractive a settlement as **Akapnou** or, further east, **Pendakomo**.

RETIREMENT HOTSPOTS

Coral Bay, just to the west of Pafos, is a sprawling holiday resort which is just that little bit less touristy than its neighbour. This makes it an attractive location for people seeking to buy who want to be close to a beach but don't mind that the best shops are a short bus ride away. Unfortunately prices in Coral Bay have been soaring recently – you are likely to have to pay around C£200,000 for a two-bed house and more than C£350,000 for a three-bed house.

Four km north of Coral Bay is **Peyia**, a large hillside village with wonderful sea views and a mixture of old and new properties. With the beach only five minutes' drive away and Pafos itself only 20 minutes' drive away it's not surprising that it has become hugely popular with the British – of a population of around 10,000 as many as 8,000 may be British which has inevitably led to Peyia being dubbed 'Little Britain.' You can pick up a studio flat for around C£32,000 or a three-bed apartment for C£145,000. Three-bed houses cost from C£200,00 upwards.

Larnaka

Population: approx.70,000.
Airport: Larnaka.

At first sight Larnaka is a dusty, down-at-heel town, which had to grow up abruptly and too fast when the events of 1974 brought a flood of refugees from Famagusta pouring in. However, it is a town that grows on you once you start to explore the back streets. The proximity of the airport is useful for trips to and from the UK and the shops (Marks & Spencer, Benetton, Mothercare, Mango) are as good as it gets on this side of the island. There are also several cinemas, and shops aimed at tourists often stock English-language novels. Much of the waterfront in the town centre has been pleasingly landscaped, and the pavement cafes, while touristy, are pleasant places to while away an evening. There is also a local marina (☎2465 3110) which is scheduled to be upgraded so that it can accommodate more passing yachts. Expat Andrew Miller certainly found that Larnaka grew on him:

We bought in Pafos first but did not research enough. Larnaka offers residents a less expensive and better quality of life as you don't have to pay tourist prices for everything, especially when socialising in bars and restaurants.

Some seafront holiday apartments are being revamped as luxurious apartments but if you look in the streets to the immediate north and south of the centre you will find a mixture of traditional bungalows, some of them large and classy, and small residential apartment blocks. There are also a few mouldering Ottoman-style town houses in dire need of restoration. However, most foreigners who have bought in Larnaka have opted to live in the immediate surrounds rather than in the town itself.

Heading west from Larnaka a good place to start looking for a property with character is **Maroni** village which has a large British contingent already in residence. **Kalavassos** and **Tokhni** are also inviting and have some sensitive tourism developments in place. Similarly remote and inviting is **Khirokiti**. However, probably the best known and most popular of the villages in Larnaka's hinterland is **Lefkara**, which, like Pafos, comes in two parts: Pano Lefkara and Kato Lefkara. Lefkara is the biggest lace-making centre in Cyprus and lives off the proceeds of this expensive cottage industry. Pano Lefkara is extremely attractive, with old stone houses lining streets too narrow for cars to pass easily. For that reason alone prices here are steep in comparison with what you would pay elsewhere.

Heading east from Larnaka lots of villas are still going up but the coast is overdeveloped and the Dhekelia power station a real eyesore.

Ayia Napa

Population: approx 3000.

Airport: Larnaka.

Ayia Napa is where it all happens in terms of youthful sun-and-sea tourism. It's a lurid strip of bars, hotels and restaurants which seems oddly out of keeping with the generally sleepier pace of the island. This is where most of the younger foreigners who have settled in Southern Cyprus have found their home.

Recently the Cypriots have tired of the riotous goings-on and the inevitable lurid publicity overseas and things are quietening down, not least because fashion is fickle and other Mediterranean resorts are now more popular than Ayia Napa. The local authority has also invested money in landscaping and the sort of facilities, including a marine museum and a water theme park, that attract families rather than single holidaymakers. They have also clamped down on pub opening hours and unsightly adverts in an attempt to reposition the town more upmarket. In the short-term, however, it is not a place where those in search of the 'real' Cyprus would want to settle.

People who have enjoyed holidays in Ayia Napa but don't want to live in the town sometimes opt to buy in villages just a few miles inland such as **Liopetri, Avgorou** and **Frenaros** where developers are busily at work creating more villas

If you are considering buying a holiday home to rent out for part of the year you should bear in mind that Ayia Napa effectively closes down out of season. Oddly enough, it still receives a large number of visitors in the off-season, most of them older holidaymakers on long-stay packages.

The proximity of Cape Greco nature reserve could be a big selling point if you want to rent out your property. It is only a short drive out of town although the scenery is marred by an ugly radio mast.

Paralimni

Population: 3,500
Airport: Larnaka

Paralimni is a sleepy small town that grew enormously after 1974 when the residents of Famagusta were forced to feel south. Today it spreads out from a central square dominated by a vast modern church and two smaller ones. There's an amphitheatre, several inviting tavernas, the start of a café society and some decent shops including a branch of Marks & Spencer and several supermarkets. Not far away the beach at **Protaras** was once beautiful but is now completely overlooked by package-holiday hotels. There are quite a few housing developments nearby and foreigners have been buying in the inland village of **Sotira.**

Note that this part of Southern Cyprus is often referred to rather confusingly as 'Ammochostos' which was the Greek name for Famagusta.

Troodos Mountains

Centres of population: *Platres, Kakopetria.*
Airport: *Larnaka.*

For many people, Cyprus's pride and joy are the Troodos Mountains where the beauty of the landscape has forced the developers to rein in their ambitions. That said, the villas are still going up, and with them the advertising hoardings promising to 'build your dream'. Most of the building is relatively sensitive, although there are a few conspicuous eyesores and some enormous villas whose size is completely at odds with the traditional architecture.

The small towns of Platres, Troodos and Kakopetria are not, perhaps, the idyllic, unspoilt communities you might expect. However, there are many smaller villages which are largely deserted as young people leave in search of work in the coastal towns. In these places a foreigner can still buy a ruined cottage and turn it into a home full of character. However, so far few have shown much interest in doing so.

Platres is the most readily accessible of the Troodos towns and stays fairly cool even in high summer. However, that is also when it becomes jam-packed with day-trippers every weekend. Quite a lot of new development has taken place here, much of it to house expat Russians. Troodos itself is much less appealing, consisting as it does of a purpose-built resort complex which is mobbed with day-trippers. Kakopetria is more two-faced, with a pleasingly restored old quarter rubbing shoulders with some truly out-of-place high-rise hotels. Many Kakopetrians spend most of the year in London and then come back to their 'village' in summer.

Finding somewhere to buy in any of these places is probably as much to do with who you know and having an ear to the ground as relying on an estate agent to do the legwork for you. Those in the know suggest that you look for a home in a village ideally located midway between the humidity belt of the coast and the snowline of the mountains. If you don't know where to start looking for the owner of an abandoned property try asking the local *muktar* or village headman.

The European Regional Development Fund has just announced a project to revive 15 villages, some of them in the Troodos. Fifty per cent of the money will come from the ERDF, with another 40% coming from the Cypriot government and the final 10% from the villages themselves.

Polis

Airport: Pafos.

It may not be the quiet hippy hangout it once was but unlike the resorts of the south coast, Polis, on the northern side of the Akamas Peninsula, has managed to hang on to some of its old laidback charm, especially in the pedestrianised town center with its pleasant tavernas. Plenty of British people have already settled in Polis and the nearby seaside resort of **Latsi** and there seem to be more people with an interest in doing up old houses or building their own house in this part of the island.

East of Polis new villa developments are going up at the usual high speed although the road east is quickly cut off by the Attila Line separating it from the North Cypriot town of Güzelyurt (Morfou).

Lefkosia (Nicosia)

Population: approx. 200,000
Airport: Larnaka

Lefkosia is a bustling modern city sprawling south from the old walled town at its heart which is where the limited tourism action can be found in the restored quarter of Laiki Yitonia. Its inland location deprives Lefkosia of cooling sea breezes and in summer it can be overwhelmingly hot. However, this is definitely the place to come for the widest range of shops and cultural life on the island. As Graham Colville summed it up:

I wouldn't live anywhere else. All the culture is here, and the Moufflon Bookshop. For the first time in my life I live in the heart of things and am free of the tyranny of the motor car. Of course in the summer we sizzle.

Lefkosia is more cosmopolitan than you might expect, with a large semi-resident population of Russians, Sri Lankans, Lebanese, Iranians, Turks, Syrians and Kurds. It was forced to grow rapidly and haphazardly in 1974 as refugees flooded in from the north but most of that growth took place to the south of the fascinating old town. This is where you'll find the main shopping streets, with high-street names like Debenhams, Next, Mothercare and Zara in evidence.

For the time being Lefkosia remains blighted by the Atilla Line which runs through it, cutting streets off so abruptly that windows actually overhang the no man's land beyond. This is a shame since it means that few foreigners have wanted to buy properties even in the attractive **Chrysaliniotissa** area which has some fine stone houses with lovely tiled floors and inviting courtyards. This part of town, nestling within the Venetian walls and slap up against the Atilla Line, is being restored by UNDP and UNHCS as part of the Nicosia Master Plan. Should peace ever break out this would be the area in which to buy, especially as it is close to the Famagusta Gate area which has some of the town's most popular bars and cafés. For the time being though it is a strange mix, with pockets of UN-subsidised gentrification rubbing up against complete dereliction. A few young families have been lured back into the area with subsidised rents, although they complain about the lack of parking space available. Note that some buildings that look original are in fact exact replicas of old buildings that were in too poor a condition to restore.

The one other part of Lefkosia which has old properties for sale is the suburb of **Kaimakli** where many villas and townhouses were built by wealthy local stonemasons. It's a strange, introspective suburb where no one speaks English, but the cement mixers rumbling through the narrow streets and the odd incongruous swimming pool suggest that gentrification is already well underway.

Properties for Sale in Southern Cyprus

Location	Type	Description	Price
Pafos	Apartment	One bedroom/two bedroom	C£57,500/ C£76,000
Pafos	Villa	Three bedrooms. Swimming pool	C£139,000
Fyti village near Pafos	Restored village cottage	Two bedrooms	C£110,000
Lemesos town	Apartment	Two bedrooms	C£82,000
Trimiklini, village near Lemesos	Bungalow	One bedroom	C£40,000
Germasogeia, large village Lemesos area	Detached house	Three bedrooms	C£298,000
Kiti, near Larnaka	Detached house	Four bedrooms	C£150,000
Larnaka	Apartment	Four bedrooms	C£140,000
Kiti, near Larnaka	Detached house	Five bedrooms. Pool.	£195,000

NORTHERN CYPRUS

Lefkoşa

Population: 39,000
Airport: Ercan International

While Lefkosia bustles, Lefkoşa, the southern half of old Nicosia, simply snoozes. It is a real backwoods town that seems to be becoming even sleepier as most of the tourism and property development action focuses on Girne. Lefkoşa could be any small town on the Turkish mainland were it not for the scattering of fine medieval buildings that pay homage to its past as the capital of the Lusignan kings. Forget exciting shopping – this may be the capital of the TRNC but so far it has little to show for that accolade.

Not surprisingly few foreigners have shown much interest in buying property in Lefkoşa. Were they to do so the most interesting area is probably **Arabahmet**. Like Chrysaliniotissa in Lefkosia, this quarter is full of fine stone townhouses which have been restored as part of the Nicosia Master Plan. However, as with Chrysaliniotissa, Arabahmet abuts against the Green Line and overlooks no man's land which means that few Brits would want to buy there until such time as a peace plan is worked out. In the meantime many of these wonderful old houses are filled with refugees and poor settlers from the east of Turkey. The few foreigners who have already bought houses to restore in Arabahmet are doing so under supervision so careful that one Italian who had imported fine new floor tiles reportedly came back to find them concreted over as 'inappropriate'.

One other area of Lefkoşa has also been restored. The **Samanbahçe** neighbourhood is very near the Kyrenia Gate in the town centre. Its neat streets of tiny houses open straight onto streets that radiate from a central fountain. They look cute but are too small to interest most foreign buyers.

Girne (Kyrenia)

Population: 12,000
Airports: Ercan International, Lefkoşa

Girne has one of the prettiest harbours in the entire Mediterranean, with fine stone buildings ringing the waterfront and the vast walls of a medieval castle nestling beneath the craggy backdrop of the Kyrenia Mountains. Although most of the harbour buildings now house fish restaurants and/or hotels unsightly development has been kept at bay and only palm trees dare challenge the minaret of the local mosque for primacy on the skyline. Beyond the harbour Girne has a few pleasant shopping streets, a handful of small hotels, a variety of restaurants, including some serving Indian cuisine, a terminal for shared taxis to Lefkoşa and Mağusa and some grand early 20th-century buildings housing the National Archives, the Land Registry and other government offices. Afterwards comes the familiar sprawl of new building that can be seen all over the island. You need to drive almost to Güzelyalı in the west and Arapköy in the east before you are clear of the sprawl of 'luxury villas'.

Girne had a long history as the retirement home of choice for the British and by 1974 there were already around 2,500 Brits living here, making up roughly half the town's population. Nowadays, however, most of the people who have been snapping up homes locally are actually buying in the surrounding countryside and in the villages in the foothills of the spectacularly craggy Kyrenia Mountains. Decades ago Lawrence Durrell immortalised pretty little Beylerbeyi (Bellapais) with its picturesque ruined abbey by writing about his experiences as one of the first expats to buy a house, restore it and settle there in his *Bitter Lemons*. Those who have come after him have been less interested in restoring old properties and more interested in buying new-built villas and apartments in the outskirts.

Villages where development is currently forging ahead include **Esentepe, Edremit, Alsancak, Arapköy, Karşıyaka, Çatalköy, Ozanköy, Tatlısu, Bahçeli** and **Lapta**, some of them little more than extensions of the Girne sprawl. When choosing a property in one of these settlements it is vital to think about further developments that might take place and which might wreck the view for which you bought your property.

At one time **Karaman** (Karmi) was *the* place to buy, with the government arranging 25-year leases on all the properties there for foreign buyers only. The village was intrinsically pretty and became more so as expats, most of them British and German, did up the whitewashed cottages. However, it was never a very lively place and now many of the houses are in search of new owners. Potential incomers would do well to bear in mind the essential political conservatism of most of those already settled in Karaman.

Lapta is one of the more inviting villages, with the added advantage of a reliable water supply. The government also leased houses to foreigners here but as their 25-year leases are running out, so some seem keen to sell and go.

Future plans that might influence you in deciding whether to buy in Girne itself include expansion of the Delta Marina and a bypass to alleviate the worsening traffic problem. At the time of writing a lot of improvements were being made to the old part of town immediately above the harbour. Recobbling some of the streets is making them less comfortable to walk on but certainly looks prettier than concreting them over. Funding for this work is coming from the EU via UNDP but at the same time private individuals are doing up some of the old stone houses under the careful supervision of the conservation authorities. The end result should be an even more inviting centre to the town.

RETIREMENT HOTSPOT

The contiguous villages of **Lapta, Alsancak** and **Karşıyaka** in the foothills of the Kyrenia Mountains have proved particularly popular with retirees, no doubt because they are close enough to Girne to benefit from town amenities but far enough out to escape the noise and traffic congestion. Lapta was a historic settlement and so the village has a real centre, with shops, small restaurants and a post office. There are a few pleasant old properties available but most people opt for new-build villas with sea and mountain views. To buy a new-build three-bedroom villa in Lapta is likely to cost you around £125,000.

Gazimağusa (Famagusta)

Population: 27,000

Airport: Ercan International, Lefkoşa

Gazimağusa (the old Famagusta, now Mağusa in everyday talk) is a striking port town, much of it still enclosed within sturdy medieval walls that are said to have inspired Shakespeare's *Othello*. The area inside the walls is like one vast open-air museum of European medieval architecture with its crowning glory the magnificent Gothic cathedral, now a mosque. This square has become the focus for a sustained attempt to revitalise the town, with several inviting pavement cafés gathered round the pedestrianised town square and the EU pouring money into the restoration of the old municipal market buildings to house chi-chi shops.

RETIREMENT HOTSPOT

Boğaz was, just a few years ago, a handful of bungalows overlooking a beach. However, as people have started to discover the east coast of Northern Cyprus so this blink-and-you'll-miss-it settlement is rapidly swelling. Boğaz's appeal lies in its location which is handy for the bright lights of Gazimağusa and for the as yet unspoilt beaches of the Karpaz Peninsula. For anyone with mobility problems it must also help that the area is generally very flat. Taken individually, the villas going up here are often attractive although *en masse* they are less appealing. Expect to pay around £60,000 for a two-bed flat or £100,000 for a three-bed house.

Given how attractive old Mağusa is, it is perhaps surprising that foreigners have been slow to snap up properties here as they have done in Girne. However, there is a dark side to the story which is the ghost settlement of Maraş (Varosha) which stretches away to the south of the walled city. Before 1974 this was one of Cyprus's prime tourist centres, a Benidorm-lookalike of high-rise hotels catering to the mass market. Now, however, it stands in limbo, its hotels abandoned to the occasional UN visitor. Until a peace settlement finally sorts out what is going to happen to Maraş it is unlikely that many people will feel confident enough to settle in this area.

However, in the last couple of years foreigners have started to buy properties in the town centre, with older properties in need of restoration the purchases of choice. A few people have also bought north of Mağusa, especially around the sandy beach at **Boğaz** and around the Roman ruins at **Salamis**; the first estate agencies to cater for them have now opened in Mağusa town centre. Otherwise there still seem to be few takers either here or further east on the unspoilt Karpaz Peninsula, where some of the few remaining Greek-Cypriot residents of the north live.

The Arestis Case

In 2005 Greek Cypriot Myra Xenides-Arestis applied to the European Court of Human Rights, claiming that Turkey had violated her human rights by failing to allow her to return to her family home in Maraş/Varosha. The court ruled in her favour and ordered Turkey to find a way of resolving the problem, although it didn't order Ankara to pay her compensation. A further 1,400 similar cases have been waiting for the final outcome of the Arestis case.

Turkey has set up a committee to consider its response but it is hard to see what it can do other than return the area to the Greek Cypriots to avoid paying anyone compensation; or hand administration of the area to the TRNC and let the Greek Cypriots return home under their authority. It has been suggested that the TRNC could set up a committee to run the area and gradually replace the Turkish Cypriots on it with Greek Cypriots as more of them returned until eventually Maraş/Varosha became an autonomous region under TRNC sovereignty. It's a nice idea but seems somewhat utopian when the two sides can so rarely agree on the simplest things.

Güzelyurt (Morphou)

Population: 12,865
Airports: Ercan International, Lefkoşa

Way out to the west of the island, Güzelyurt is a sleepy small town whose winding narrow streets were clearly laid out in the days when cars were a rarity. It's a town of low-rise buildings, some of them fading but graceful Art Deco villas, others imposing pilastered edifices which date from the Greek Revival period of the late 19th and early 20th century. However, you could be forgiven for assuming that the entire place has hardly seen a lick of paint since 1974.

Not many foreigners would want to live in Güzelyurt. However, it is a transport and shopping centre for the surrounding villages and, as such, likely to pay an important part in the lives of retirees settling in the area. It also has a 9-hole golf course, although you should not expect anything as lavish as in Southern Cyprus. Anyone considering buying here should bear in mind the Güzelyurt Economic Development Plan which covers 12,000 donums to the north of town, 880 of which will be distributed to young families to create homes and some of which will be used for tourism. A dual carriageway to link the new campus of the Middle East Technical University at Kalkanlı to Güzelyurt is also in the pipeline.

More foreigners have taken up residence in **Lefke**, a pretty hillside settlement surrounded by orange orchards. It would be hard to imagine anywhere sleepier than this, although there are some lovely old shuttered mansions and even a few brick houses that manage to look like an English terrace. Gardens echo with birdsong and are full of orange and lemon trees, soaring palms and banks of prickly pear bushes. There is a pleasant small hotel for when friends come to stay, and the ruins of Soli and Vouna a short drive away. A few foreign followers of the Sufi leader Kıbrıslı Şeyh Nazim have taken up residence here.

İskele (Trikomo)

Population: 2,800
Airport: Ercan International, Lefkoşa

North of Mağusa the flat coastal plain leading to the Karpaz Peninsula is being steadily developed with endless mix-and-match villas, mostly cut off from the sea by the main road. The 'town' of İskele itself is tiny and unlikely to appeal to retirees. However, north of it the village of Boğaz has taken off in a big way, despite being very small with only a handful of restaurants and a couple of shops to its name. The talk is of development even further north at Bafra on the fringes of the Karpaz Peninsula, a good or bad thing depending on your point of view.

Typical properties for sale in Northern Cyprus

Location	Type	Description	Price
Girne	City centre apartment with shared pool	Three bedrooms	£50,000
Alsancak	Villa	Three bedrooms	£115,000
Upper Kyrenia	New apartment	Three bedrooms. 5 minutes from city centre. Sea and mountain views.	£60,000
Lapta	Bungalow in development of three	Three bedrooms. Communal pool. Sea views	£70,000
Beylerbeyi (Bellapais, nr Girne)	Apartment with shared pool.	Two bedrooms.	£75,000

Useful Contact for Northern Cyprus

North Cyprus Properties: www.northcyprusproperties.co.uk. Website of organisation that supports potential buyers looking for properties in northern Cyprus. Databases of properties for sale, lawyer list and other useful information.

Your New Home in Cyprus

CHAPTER SUMMARY

- **Construction,** especially of three-bed villas, is speeding ahead all over the island.
- **Prices are rising fast** in Northern *and* Southern Cyprus.
- There are **plenty of estate agents** to help you find a property. Those in Southern Cyprus are legally required to be licenced.
- If you visit Cyprus on an estate-agent-sponsored **inspection trip** you should take care not to let yourself be rushed into buying anything.
- There are plenty of **villas and apartments** for sale. Although some people choose to restore **older properties,** this can be more expensive than buying a new-build home.
- Many people buy **off-plan properties** and some sell them straight on again at a profit before they have actually lived in them.
- Because of Cyprus's **complicated political history** it is vital to find out the **exact legal ownership of any property** as shown on the title deed before agreeing to buy.
- The **buying process** is not dissimilar to its UK equivalent. However, you may wait years to obtain your title deed.
- Although Cyprus is extremely hot for much of the year you do need **heating** for the winter. **Air conditioning** is virtually essential to be comfortable in the summer.
- Getting a **new phone line** installed can be frustratingly slow. In the north many people make do with mobile phones.
- Much of the **rental accommodation** available is in self-catering package-holiday units.

OVERVIEW OF THE CYPRIOT PROPERTY MARKET

The last few years have seen property prices in Cyprus soaring. Two main factors have contributed to this. In the run-up to the the Republic of Cyprus's accession to the EU the property market took off dramatically, especially in the north, as investors rushed to beat predictions of even higher prices when one or both parts of the island joined the Union. At the same time booming house prices in the UK encouraged more and more people to sell up or trade down and invest in new homes in Cyprus. The combined effect of these two pressures was that in parts of Southern Cyprus prices rose by 25% in 2004 and the same again in 2005, while during the last six months of 2003 prices in Northern Cyprus doubled, only to do the same again in 2004.

By 2006 price increases had slowed down as more and more new properties flooded the market and as stagnating UK house prices made it harder for people to sell up and leave. Higher house prices in Cyprus also meant that the huge price differential between the UK and Cyprus had started to close, making it harder for people to buy a house on the island and bank enough to see them through their retirement.

That said, the cost of land (as opposed to property) is still rising at about 20% per year in the south and could continue to do so for some time to come as Cypriots move into buying land instead of buildings. Prices in the north are still considerably cheaper than those in the south but will probably keep on rising. Should the two parts of the country ever reunite it is likely that prices will level off, with those in the south falling slightly and those in the north rising still further.

This might suggest that buying in the north is likely to prove a good investment. However, a word of warning is necessary for anyone thinking of buying property there. Because of the population exchange that occurred in 1974, many Cypriots are refugees either within their own country or abroad. A question mark, therefore, hangs over the precise ownership of many properties and pieces of land. It is true that some refugees have long since given up hope of returning to their original homes and have elected to sell them to foreigners. However, a situation like this leaves the field wide open for unscrupulous property speculators. Until there is a final settlement in Cyprus **it is imperative that anyone wishing to buy there takes good, independent legal**

advice before proceeding; taking the word of a 'friend' or even a friendly estate agent as to the precise legal ownership of a property could lead to expense and heartache later. Although this is also true in Southern Cyprus it is more of a burning issue in the north.

Property development has become one of the biggest industries on the island. Everywhere you look new developments are going up, and one more thing to be wary of is the very real risk that the north will end up just as over-developed as many would argue the south already is. Some of this building is purely speculative, with buyers hoping to buy off-plan, then sell on again at a profit without ever living in the property. Of course their behaviour helps push up prices for everyone. Arguably it also encourages sloppy building, since a speculator has little incentive to supervise the building work to ensure it reaches the highest standards.

So far most foreign settlers in Cyprus have been more interested in buying new properties than in restoring old ones. However, in Lefkosia/ Lefkoşa there are some fine old houses left over from Ottoman times which are crying out for owners who can afford to modernise them. In rural areas there are also still some tumbledown stone cottages, often with very rudimentary facilities, for sale, although few estate agents seem interested in advertising them. In northern Cyprus a typical ruinous village property is likely to cost around £50,000 to buy but would-be owners would need to budget at least another £25,000 to cover the cost of restoration. In the south you would probably have to budget at least twice those amounts, although there are still tiny cottages that go for as little as C£45,000.

The village of Karaman (Karmi) in Northern Cyprus offers a cautionary tale for would-be buyers. All the houses there were once advertised for sale to foreigners on 25-year leases. Now, of course, the leases are almost up and their holders are unable to convert them in freeholds. Consequently, despite its beauty, Karaman has fallen from favour as a place to live.

The sheer volume of new construction in Cyprus means that it may eventually become a buyer's market, with not enough would-be purchasers to keep prices high. It is already obvious that local people are being priced out of the market in the same way that first-time-buyers are in the UK. In such circumstances there must be a risk that the bubble will burst and bring prices down again. For people wanting to retire to Cyprus and buying without a mortgage this may not be such a disaster but for speculators it could be. In 2006 the properties that were selling fastest were those at the cheaper end of the market but there were ominous rumblings about houses sitting on the market for up to a year before finding a buyer.

There also seems to be something of a mismatch between what the developers want to build (i.e. three-bedroomed luxury villas) and the needs of a typical retired couple who might be better off with something considerably smaller and lower maintenance.

At the moment EU citizens are free to buy one property of up to three donums (4,014 sq. m) in **Southern Cyprus** on the same terms as a local; a husband and wife can only buy one property between them (and it is not possible to buy as joint owners except as husband and wife), although different rules apply for purchases made through a company. However, from May 2009 EU citizens will be able to buy as many properties as they like. In **Northern Cyprus** the rules stipulate only one property per surname – a requirement easily circumvented by judicious use of friends and relatives.

A Cautionary Tale

In 2005 a court case involving a property in Lapta exemplified the dangers of buying in Northern Cyprus without very careful advice as to the legality of the purchase. The Orams from Hove had spent around £160,000 on building a villa with a swimming pool on a piece of land there. However, in April 2005 a court in Southern Cyprus ordered that they must take it down and return the land to its original Greek Cypriot owner together with £10,000 in compensation. Although the court had no authority to enforce this ruling in Northern Cyprus, lawyers for the displaced owner registered the judgment with the British High Court under European law which says that a judgment in one EU member country can be enforced in another. At the time of writing a final decision was still awaited but if the lawyers win the case the Orams could find their assets in the UK up for grabs in settlement. The Orams have challenged the ruling, arguing that they bought the land in good faith from a displaced Turkish Cypriot. If they lose, their case could set a precedent for deciding other such disputes on a case by case basis. However, it is likely that the British courts will decide that it is against public policy to recognize the ruling in the UK courts - which could give a green light for the development of many properties in disputed ownership.

FINDING A PROPERTY

The English-language newspapers published in north and south Cyprus are a good source of information about estate agents, house prices and general issues to do with buying property on the island. Properties in Cyprus also feature in all the UK property shows and the Karaolis Group specialises in shows featuring Southern Cyprus. However, there is no substitute for research on the ground. You should take your time and visit as many properties as you can, taking photographs as you go so that you will remember which was which. When comparing prices make sure you are comparing like with like since different agents will measure properties in different ways, some of them including things like balconies in their measurements while others do not.

The Internet

Increasingly estate agents and property developers use the web as a relatively cheap marketing tool and a way to get their name known internationally. Some internet portals feature properties for sale with thousands of agents and developers. Using a search engine such as www.google.co.uk will lead you to websites dealing solely with Cypriot properties. Sites worth looking at, especially for those planning to buy at the top end of the market, are Knight Frank (www.knightfrank.com), www.primelocation.com, www.propertyfinder.com, and www.newskys.co.uk.

> Because of the quantity of information (as well as misinformation and downright junk) posted on the internet you will need to narrow down your search using a web directory or search engine. For example, rather than just typing in 'property, Cyprus' or 'villas for sale, Cyprus', name the specific area or town where you want to buy. If you know the name of a property developer or estate agent with whom you are thinking of doing business, then use the web as a research tool to find out as much as you can about them. You can make initial contact with vendors of properties which interest you by using e-mail (get a free e-mail address at www.hotmail.com or yahoo.co.uk) but if you decide to continue with negotiations it is best to set up a face-to-face meeting.

Property Exhibitions and Seminars

The property exhibitions held in the UK and Ireland offer an opportunity to make contact with estate agents and property developers specialising in the overseas market. Occasional seminars are also given on the Cypriot property market. Exhibitors tend to deal primarily with the most popular areas so if you're looking for something unusual a property exhibition may have little to offer you.

Exhibition Organisers

Homes Overseas: ☎020-7002 8300; www.blendoncommunications.com.

Homebuyer Events Ltd: ☎020-8877 3636; www.homebuyer.co.uk.

International Property Show: ☎01252-720652; www.internationalpropertyshow.com.

Karaolis Group: www.karaolisgroup.com.

World Class Homes: ☎01582-832 001; www.worldclasshomes.co.uk.

To find out when and where the next property exhibition will be taking place check out www.tsnn.co.uk.

Newspapers & Magazines

Once you start looking into the possibility of buying property in Cyprus you will quickly discover the vast number of companies competing to persuade you to do business with them. Buy any of the British property or lifestyle magazines and you will find their pages crammed with advertisements placed by property developers, estate agents, removals firms, lawyers, insurers and accountants. The property pages of the weekend newspapers also carry articles on buying property abroad which feature sample property prices and estate agent details.

In Cyprus itself many estate agents advertise in *Cyprus Today, Cyprus Mail* (www.cyprus-mail.com) and *Cyprus Weekly* (www.cyprusweekly.com.cy). However, the prices advertised in Greek and Turkish Cypriot newspapers are sometimes lower than those in the English-language papers so it is worth asking a Greek or Turkish-reading friend to keep an eye out for you.

In Northern Cyprus the monthly *Kızey Turizm* (North Tourism) magazine also contains advertisements for estate agents and information about local property development.

British Property Magazines

A Place in the Sun: ☎01342-828700; www,channel4.com/life/microsites/A/a_place_in_the_sun.

Homes Overseas: ☎020-7939 9888; www.blendoncommunications.com.

Cypriot Property Magazines & Newspapers

Cyprus Property & Home: : ☎2573 0203;; email cyprop@spidernet.com.cy.

Paphos Property Gazette: ☎2693 3775.

Property Nc Magazine: http://propertync.com/.

Other magazines include: Kuzey Kıbrıs Home, My Property Cyprus.Com, Property & Home Cyprus, Your Home in the Sun.

Estate Agents

Cypriot Estate Agents. Over the last few years it has sometimes seemed as if every man and his dog was setting up business as an estate agent on Cyprus. For example, as recently as 2003 Girne had more than 100 estate agents, and in Pafos it still sometimes feels as if every building that is not a restaurant is an estate agency. However, as the market has slowed down some of the agencies in the north have closed down, while in the south matters have been brought under control to some extent by a new law in 2004 which imposed obligations on would-be estate agents. The Cyprus Real Estate Agents Association (☎2693 4055; www.ccci.org.cy) has the details but certainly you can now ask to see an estate agent's licence before agreeing to work with them.

Although some people hope to save money by looking for a property without using an estate agent, the vast majority do use one, and most agents in both the north and the south operate in much the same way as those in the UK. Their windows are full of cards showing attractive properties, either already built or in the making, together with details of their dimensions, what they have to offer and the asking price. Sometimes it may turn out that the advertised price is as fictional as the cheap holiday offers in UK travel agency windows. However, browsing the estate agents' windows is likely to give you a good idea what to expect.

With so many agents flooding the market you would be well advised to ask other expats which ones they have used in order to find someone trustworthy and knowledgeable. In Southern Cyprus many agents have grouped together to advertise themselves on the internet; try www.buyrentcyprus.com or www.findaproperty.co.uk.

The Importance of a Good Estate Agent

In the particular case of Cyprus it is especially advisable to use a reputable agent in order to avoid the pitfall of buying a property whose ownership is questionable. A good Cypriot estate agent will help the buyer through the whole buying process, from negotiating with the seller to organising builders and renovators; some will even help you order locally-made furniture.

Unlike in the UK the line between estate agencies and construction companies is often blurred. Good estate agents often undertake to oversee building work on your property and normally factor into the contract a penalty clause in case the work falls behind schedule. If you cut out the estate agent there is every chance that you will have problems with your builders. On the other hand if you deal directly with a developer you could save having to pay the estate agent's commission.

As in the UK the agent acts primarily for the vendor so you should always take independent legal advice even if they recommend a solicitor. While the agent will have a vested interest in recommending a lawyer who will get everything sorted out as quickly as possible they may be working too closely with the agent to be able to put your interests first when a problem arises. They may also charge more than a solicitor you find yourself.

June and Jeremy Hall bought a plot of land in Lapta in Northern Cyprus. They had very few problems and said:

'We liked our estate agent and the builder – the agent had lived in Australia and his sons spoke English which certainly helped. It's very important to get an independent solicitor (although it's tricky because everyone is related!) and a quality builder.'

British Estate Agents. Some British estate agents act as middlemen for Cypriot agents. Because they have an office in the UK, such agencies often make a good starting place for finding out what is available. However, simply being British does not guarantee that an agent is reputable – always take advice from other people who have already bought in your area before committing yourself. Dealing with a Cyprus-based estate agent directly may turn out to be much cheaper than using a British middleman.

Useful Contacts

National Association of Estate Agents: ☎01926-496800; www.naea.co.uk.

Royal Institute of Chartered Surveyors: ☎0870-333 1600; www.rics.org.

European Confederation of Real Estate Agents: www.webcei.com.

The Federation of Overseas Property Developers, Agents & Consultants: ☎0870-3501223; www.fopdac.com.

Commission. Different estate agencies sometimes charge different commissions. You usually pay a higher rate of commission for a cheap property than for a more expensive one, and the rate may also vary from region to region, with higher rates being charged in the most popular areas. Usually you should expect to pay around 3% of the purchase price in commission.

Estate Agents for Northern Cyprus

Arch Property Development & Construction Company: ☎815 8709; e-mail alkin@arch-cyprus-properties.com; 67 Ziya Rızkı Caddesi, Girne.

Frost Property Services: ☎366 9606; www.frostpropertyservices.com; Dukkan 29, Celalettin Sokak, Mağusa.

Ian Smith Estate Agents: ☎815 7118; fax 0392-815 7119; www.iansmithestate.com; opposite Ship Hotel, Girne-Lapta road, Girne.

Invest & Prosper: ☎816 0444, www.investandprosperproperties.com; Namık Kemal Caddesi, Kalnar İş Merkezi 5, Girne.

Nokta Construction & Estate Agents: ☎822 3528; www.noktaestates.com; Terkan Plaza 5, Girne-Lapta road, Girne.

North Cyprus Properties: ☎815 5453, www.north-cyprus-properties.com; Girne.

Remax: ☎815 5885, www.remax-golden.com; 46 Ziya Rızkı St, Girne.

Sunny Property Estate Agents: ☎0161-233 0400; www.sunny-property.co.uk; Peel House, 30 The Downs, Altrincham, Cheshire, WA14 2PX;. Address in Northern Cyprus: ☎+90 392 815 7791; 2 Kemal Paşa Sokak, Lefkoşa.

Estate Agents for Southern Cyprus

Andreas Foutas Estates: ☎252 1058, www.clickforcyprusproperty.com; Pissouri village.

Antonis Loizou & Associates: UK freephone 0800 0326203; ☎2587 1552. www.aloizou.com.cy. Surveyors, architects, marketing and property sales throughout Cyprus. Go to www.aloizpou.com/contacts.htm for a list of offices in Cyprus or contact Halcyon Properties (see below).

Aresti Estate Agency Ltd: ☎2691 2100; www.aresti-realestate.com; 7/26 Tombs of the Kings Road, Pafos. Sales and rentals, Pafos area.

Benacon: www.benacon.com; 75 Archbishop Makarios III Avenue, Pafos. Estate agents, builders, engineers and architects group. Pafos area.

BuySell Cyprus: ☎0800 00222, www.BuySellCyprus.com. Chain agency with offices all over Southern Cyprus.

Capital Growth Real Estate Agents Ltd: ☎2481 7711; www.cgestates.com; Shop 14, Frixos Business Centre, 33 Arch. Makarios Ave III, Larnaka. Range of properties in Ayia Napa, Lemesos, Lefkosia and Pafos.

Coopers Overseas: ☎01895-812233, www.coopersoverseas.co.uk; 109 Hillingdon Hill, Hillingdon, Uxbridge UB10 0NR. Family-run estate agency which specialises in Cyprus.

Halcyon Properties: ☎01273-208225; www.halcyonproperties.co.uk; 3 Dukes Close, Seaford, East Sussex BN25 2TU. British Associate company for Anthony Loizou & Associates Cyprus estate agents. Contacts in all main towns and resorts.

Knight Frank: ☎020-7861 1060, www.knightfrank.com. Upmarket property specialist.

My Property Cyprus Real Estate: ☎2381 4477, www.mypropertycyprus.com. Sells properties all over Southern Cyprus.

Premier Resorts: ☎020-8940 9406, www.premierresorts.co.uk, Upmarket property speciliast. Deals with Aphrodite Hills.

Peter Stephenson Properties: ☎2682 2277; www.peterstephenson.co.uk 15 Apostolou Pavlou Avenue, Pafos. Properties in Pafos and Lemesos.

Property Developers in Southern Cyprus

If you want to buy an off-plan or brand-new property direct from the developer you may be able to save money on estate agent's fees as well as on legal fees as most developers will have pro-forma contracts that they use for all their homes. These are some of the largest firms of property developers in Southern Cyprus:

Aristo Developers: ☎2693 2088; www.aristodevelopers.com.
Cybarco: ☎020-8371 9700; www.cybarco.com.
Kleanthis Savva: ☎2681 5444; www.ksavva-developers.com.
Leptos Estates: ☎2688 0100; www.leptosestates.com.
Pafilia Property Developers: ☎0800-6106; www.pafilia.com.
Quality Developers: ☎2466 2333; www.qualitydevelopments.com.

Property Developer in Northern Cyprus

The following company is the leading developer in North Cyprus, specialising in gated complexes of luxury apartments.

SeaTerra Cyprus: ☎392 816 0140; UK landline freephone ☎0800 849 4168; www.Cyprus-seaterra.com.

Questions to Ask Before Selecting a Developer

- What other projects have they worked on? Go and take a look to assess the quality of the workmanship.
- Does the company own the freehold on the land it plans to develop?

- Does it have building permission for the project?
- Is there a title deed for the unit you want to buy? If the land has only one deed that will have to be divided later this can result in long delays before you get your individual deed.
- What bank does the company use?
- How many staff are working for the company?

Inspection Trips

Some estate agents in both Northern and Southern Cyprus will arrange inspection trips to help you find a suitable property. Typically, the estate agency books the flight, collects you from and returns you to the airport, and provides free accommodation for the duration of your trip. A consultant will take you round various properties, showing you the area and facilities on offer. Normally you only have to pay for your flights (the price will depend on whether you are booked with a charter airline or a more expensive scheduled airline) and these will be refundable if you eventually buy a property from the agent.

HOW TO COME OUT ON TOP OF AN INSPECTION TRIP

- Have a clear idea what you are looking for in terms of size, location and price, and let the agents know before they arrange your trip.
- Don't let yourself be rushed by the agent. Take your time and be sure that you get a complete picture of all the properties that they show you.
- Try to get time away from the agent to explore on your own. If they insist that you spend your entire visit under their supervision, you are better off just walking away.
- Avoid group inspections since you will waste valuable time looking at properties that someone else wants.
- If you decide to buy a property while on an inspection trip it may be difficult to retain a lawyer other than the one the agent recommends. Remember that it is always advisable to use an independent lawyer that you have found yourself.

Although you are under no obligation to buy on these inspection trips, you may end up *feeling* obligated. Since the inspection trip means that the agent is investing time and money in you it may not be easy just to walk away. Don't allow yourself to be rushed into a decision you may regret – buying a property overseas is just as much of a big deal as it is at home.

One tip – if you decide to organise your own inspection trip try and avoid the weekend since most shops will be closed and you will not get a very realistic picture of what the area has to offer.

WHAT TYPE OF PROPERTY?

Whether your tastes run to a luxury villa with pool and sea view or to a ruinous village farmhouse, you are bound to be able to find something suitable in Cyprus. But buying a property is an investment in your future and you should be absolutely sure that it is exactly what you want before committing yourself. It is easy to get swept up in the excitement and agree to buy something completely impractical that will eat up your savings or turn out to be in the wrong place. It is vital to consider the cost of running and maintaining any property that catches your eye. Buying an apartment in a block of flats may not sound as romantic as buying an old olive farm but may turn out to be more realistic financially, with some of the maintenance costs shared with other owners. You also need to bear in mind how close you are to important amenities, especially given the scarcity of public transport.

The current building boom has mainly focused on villas and detached houses, even in Northern Cyprus where the mainland Turkish preference for living in high-rise apartments is less in evidence. On the whole you will only be able to buy an apartment in the centre of the main resorts or in Lefkosia/Lefkoşa.

The Donum

One initially confusing aspect of property-buying on Cyprus is that land size is still often advertised in the old Ottoman measurement, the donum. One donum is equal to 1,000 sq. m.

Villas

In Cyprus 'villa' is a generic term used to cover everything from bungalows to huge detached houses. What they have in common is that they are almost always described as 'luxurious'.

New-Build Properties. The vast majority of new-build property in Cyprus consists of villas in varying sizes, some of them stand-alone, others in complexes. Taken individually they are often attractive buildings, with large rooms and plenty of space around them. Taken overall, however, they can sometimes be very unattractive since each developer uses a design that appeals to them, regardless of what has already been built nearby.

Note that many new-build properties are sold with fixtures and furniture as part of the deal. They may be included in the price or charged for as an extra. You may want to consider whether this arrangement suits you as the furnishings may not suit your taste and often depend on who the builder has been able to do a deal with. Even if you don't want all the furniture supplied you may be happy to buy an electrical appliances package from the builder – just so long as you know what it is going to cost you. Bear in mind that if you buy all these 'extras' for one inclusive price this can mean that you need to pay a higher property transfer fee than if you bought them separately. There may also be implications for capital gains tax when you come to sell. One way round this is to have the lawyer draw up a separate furniture agreement' to cover the cost of the fixtures and fittings.

A detached villa usually sells for more than an equivalent-sized ordinary house in town but offers much greater privacy.

Resale. Some properties are already starting to return to the market in search of new buyers. Southern Cyprus also has a lot of villas that were originally built to serve a self-catering market that is now in the doldrums. The result is that it is particularly easy to pick up a pleasant modern villa with its own pool for a reasonable price. Buying a villa that has already been occupied should be as straightforward as buying something brand-new as long as the Land Registry has a record of any alterations or additions that have been made to it. If such

changes have not been registered then delays are likely to occur while negotiations take place between your lawyers and the local planning committee. If extensive alterations have been made to the villa and not registered (for example, if a large conservatory has been added or an outhouse converted into a dwelling) then you may be forced to pay a fine even though you were not responsible for the illegal work. Most villas are relatively modern and you are unlikely to have problems with connections to water, electricity, telephones or drainage.

Note that if you are buying a resale property for which the title deed has not yet been issued (an increasingly likely scenario), you may have to pay a contract cancellation fee. This should not be very much although sometimes developers who have become the registered owner of the property in order to be able to work on it try to charge an exorbitant amount.

Beware - Multiple Ownership

As in Turkey, land in Northern Cyprus is traditionally divided between all the children when someone dies. It can therefore turn out that more than one person owns the land and that not all the owners want to sell. However, this will only be a problem if you are buying an old property to restore rather than one that is being built from scratch.

Because of the particular political circumstances of Cyprus it can also be hard to track down the owners of properties who may well have left the island. In Mağusa, at the time of writing, one man was desperately trying to track down the death certificate of a relative who died in the UK; with it he would have several properties in the old town to sell; without it he has none.

Apartments

Traditionally Cypriots have not been as keen on apartment-living as other Europeans. However, in the towns there are plenty of apartments for sale, some them newly built, others 20 or 30 years old.

A great many holiday flats have been built, especially around the resorts. Although these often come onto the market at a reasonable price, they tend to be smaller and less well soundproofed than urban apartments because they were not designed to be lived in full-time. Older apartments may be sturdier but usually need some repairs or

modernisation. Your best bet will probably be an apartment on an upper floor where you will be further away from street noise and may be able to take advantage of through breezes. But think carefully before committing yourself to an upstairs apartment in a block without lifts since having to manage the stairs, especially with heavy shopping, could eventually become a liability.

The most inviting apartments are usually in smaller blocks although these may have higher communal charges. Avoid apartments above shops or restaurants unless you can live at the top, as far away from noise and smells as possible. Many disputes arise over communal heating and hot water systems so try and avoid apartments where you will not have control over your own supply (this is especially important in older blocks in Northern Cyprus since Turks usually like to have the heating on at full blast all the time).

Apartments offer a relatively cheap way to get on to the Cypriot property-owning ladder. They often come with balconies and some top-floor flats have access to roof gardens. Before buying an apartment try and gauge the thickness of the walls and how much protection they offer from the sound of potential neighbours. Flats in the town centre may be great in terms of location but very noisy during the evenings. In most resorts, seafront flats offer great views but can be terribly noisy in the height of summer. Flats are cheap to maintain and generally easy to sell on, although one-bed apartments can be slow to shift. The proximity of neighbours also means that they tend to offer greater security if you are away from home a lot.

Management Committees. Just as in the UK, apartment blocks in Southern Cyprus with five or more units have management committees to look after the maintenance of communal areas, gardens, pools etc. You are legally obliged to pay a proportionate contribution towards these costs, but, again just as in the UK, it will be the luck of the draw whether you have a management committee that does its work well or takes a more casual approach to it. The only way to find out is to ask other people who are already living in the block but this will not be an option if you are buying into an off-plan scheme.

Townhouses

Cyprus has a relatively small market for townhouses, despite the fact that the centres of most of the main towns have some wonderful old houses dating back to Ottoman times that might make great places to live in with a bit of tender, loving care. Many have imposing doorways, attractively shuttered windows, central balconies, courtyards with arched cloisters and a sequence of airy rooms with soaring ceilings. Alternatively, there are town bungalows which often come with pretty tiled roofs, neat gardens and small porticos or shady, pillared porches. These, however, tend to be designed so that the main living area is in what the British would think of as a hall with other living areas opening off on both sides.

For people interested in properties with rental potential, townhouses, whether old or new, are certainly worth considering because, unlike resort properties, they can be let all year round.

Off-Plan Properties

In a fast developing market like Cyprus's many properties go on sale before they have even been built – people buy on the basis of plans and drawings, with perhaps a visit to the site and a show home. There is nothing wrong with this as long as you take precautions to make sure you are buying from a reputable builder whose developments are finished to a high standard. However, there is obviously potential for things to go wrong with buying off-plan; at best there may be delays which mean your house is not completed when you expected it to be; at worst developers have been known to collect deposits, start work and then vanish with the money, leaving the houses unfinished and their prospective owners out of pocket (the most conspicuous example of such shenanigans recently was the case of Gary Robb – see Problems below).

> In the recent past many investors bought off-plan and sold straight on for a tax-free profit before the project's completion. However, this strategy may not work for much longer. Such is the oversupply of new-build property that it is bound to become more difficult to sell on quickly. However, people who want a retirement home rather than the chance of a quick buck can still find some good off-plan bargains.

When buying off-plan you usually put down a deposit of up to 30% of the selling price, then pay for the rest of the property in instalments as the work is completed. If a property is already partly completed when the contract is signed, you may have to pay a higher deposit.

Avoiding the Pitfalls of Buying Off-Plan

- Inevitably some properties look better on paper than they do in reality. Visit other properties already completed by the same builders to find out how well they finish their jobs.
- Delays in the building process are a fact of life and can impact on your budget if, for example, you have to rent accommodation while your house is being completed.
- Estate agents and construction companies are often economical with the truth about plans for neighbouring sites which might affect your view or comfort. Keep an ear to the ground and ask other estate agents if you have reason to suspect more building may be planned.
- Make sure an independent lawyer checks your contract before it is signed as it is hard to rectify mistakes afterwards. The contract should contain information about rights of access and should specify who has responsibility for the landscaping and utility provision. It should also make clear all additional maintenance charges.
- Make sure you get a completion agreement backed up by an insurance policy that guarantees that every aspect of the property will be professionally finished off before you move in.
- Insist that payments made before the property is completed are paid into an escrow account and that the developer cannot touch it until the property is finished. This may cost extra but the bank will guarantee your money should the developer go bust.

If work has not already started when you agree to buy an off-plan property you should expect to have to wait between a year and 18 months for completion. As soon as the property is finished you will be able to take possession of it, even if there is a delay in producing the title deed – a common scenario. Before making the final payment, have your lawyer double-check that the developer is not passing on any unexpected debts or charges, and that all the necessary permits are in place.

As soon as you take possession of the property you should check for problems and ask the developer to put them right immediately; if you don't do this it will be no good complaining about a leak or a crack some months down the line. Common problems to check for are an absence of damp-proofing, insulation or guttering, as well as inadequate drains. Some Cypriot builders also face houses with Spritz instead of render. This is not waterproof and quickly cracks.

In **Northern Cyprus** the government has started to license building inspectors to check each stage of new construction. You should, therefore, be able to get local builders to guarantee their work for between five and 25 years.

The Old Versus the New

Until recently most Cypriots had little interest in old properties and couldn't wait to move into modern housing and leave a past they associated with poverty behind them. The result was that foreigners could snap up and renovate their cast-offs; indeed people were sometimes prepared to swap an old property for a new one without money even changing hands. However, slowly tastes and incomes are changing. Many Cypriots now own second homes and want places with character to escape to at weekends or for their summer holidays. Some Cypriots who have spent many years in the UK are also coming back to the island as keen to sniff out a rural idyll as the Brits themselves.

However, it is not that easy to find old properties whose owners can be traced, especially in the north. In the town centres there are some fine old houses although many are in potentially noisy locations. Some villages also have promising old stone properties for restorers to get their teeth into. But on the whole the main market in Cyprus is centred on new-build properties. If you do want to buy something old you will find few agents interested in helping you and must expect to do a lot of the legwork yourself – which means factoring in more time to find something suitable.

Tracking down a country cottage and bringing it back to life is many people's idea of a dream, and if all goes well few things can be more satisfying than sitting down for an evening meal in a beautiful house that you have restored yourself. Unfortunately not everyone is

realistic about the amount of work restoration can involve. Renovating a property usually involves months – sometimes years – of hard work. Costs also have a habit of spiralling out of control since many old houses lack sanitation, electricity, phone lines or water – which is often why the former owners abandoned them! Unless you know what you are doing, you can find that what looked like a bargain to start with actually ends up costing you a small fortune. Trying to sort out planning and other permits for yourself can also be extremely stressful, especially if you have a poor grasp on Greek or Turkish.

In contrast, if you buy a new property you are virtually guaranteed modern design, effective plumbing and wiring, efficient heating and all mod cons. Sometimes you can even design the property yourself, and the building work will be guaranteed by the builders for 10 years. Some modern developments also offer shared sporting facilities and communal services which make them even more attractive.

Having a House Built from Scratch

Many people fantasise about buying a plot of land and building their own home, and this is certainly a possibility in Cyprus. However, it is only really an option for people with time to spare – it often takes a while to find a suitable piece of land and then you really need to be on site for much of the time to keep an eye on the work. Nor should you think of it as a cheap option. In the last few years the cost of land, as opposed to property, has soared, while the cost of materials and labour has comfortably outstripped the average level of inflation. Although you might save up to 15% by doing some of the work yourself, ultimately it will probably be more expensive to build your own home than to buy one from a developer with bulk-buying muscle. It goes almost without saying that a foreigner will pay over the odds for many things that a local will be able to negotiate down in price and unless you speak fluent Greek or Turkish you may have to pay an overseer to organise the workers and supervise buying materials for you.

Bear in mind that the process of buying a plot of land to build on will involve obtaining two separate sets of permits: one for buying the land and another for building on it.

Most people build their own homes from stone or from concrete and

stone. However, some people have also started to build timber houses, so it might be worth asking builders about that possibility too.

At the time of writing land in Southern Cyprus cost around C£450-550/sq. m.

What to Do Before Buying a Plot to Build On

- You cannot simply buy a piece of land and build on as much of it as you like. Instead local regulations will dictate what percentage of a piece of land can be built on. In a town you may be able to build on as much as 90% of a plot but in the countryside you may well have to make do with building on 5% or 10% of your land.
- Get a lawyer, an architect and a surveyor to check the plot before you buy it. Make sure you know how much land is selling for in the area you're interested in from someone other than an estate agent with a vested interest in high prices.
- Check whether the land is in a conservation area where there will be strict rules about what can and cannot be done. You also need to know if there are any public rights of way over the land or any local by-laws concerning water, hunting, grazing or harvesting rights.
- If the site lacks amenities find out from the providers how expensive it will be to install sewerage, a telephone, electricity or a water supply. You may also want to find out the cost of installing a swimming pool.
- If you are thinking of building something out of keeping with what already exists in the area try and find out if it is likely to upset the locals.
- Consult the local plan which should make clear which areas have already been developed (in which case planning permission should be relatively easy to obtain). Provided the Greek word 'ikopedo' appears on the title deed the land should be zoned for building and there shouldn't be any problems either with access or with connecting the utilities.
- Check details of adjacent plots of land and try and find out whether further development is planned. In particular you should consider whether more buildings could block your wonderful sea or mountain view.
- Check that the vendor is in possession of the title deed.

- Make sure you know the exact extents of the plot to avoid future argument. Get the boundaries marked on the title deed if they aren't already and if there is any doubt pay to have the land independently surveyed.
- Boundary disputes can quickly sour relations between neighbours. If there is an orchard or olive grove on the property ask if you have the right to harvest the crops. Check that you have the rights to water from any river or well on the land.

Only when you are happy about all the above should you consider finalising a purchase.

Applying For a Building Permit. Once you have agreed to buy the land you will need to submit the plans for the proposed building to the local planning department to obtain a building permit. It is likely to take at least two months for plans of the building project to be ready for submission to the authorities.

Builders. To get the plans drawn up ask a local developer to recommend a builder or architect (all builders in Southern Cyprus must be registered). A builder will be able to provide details of standard houses and together you can work out any variations that you would like and agree on an interior design. In Northern Cyprus, however, it is not easy to find builders who can speak good English.

Architects. Alternatively an architect/engineer can come up with an original design for you. Typically, their fee is likely to come to around 6% of the entire project cost. Although it may seem easier to deal with a British architect or with someone whose mother tongue is English, a Cypriot architect familiar with local building rules and regulations, and the local climate is likely to prove more valuable in the long run.

The architect's fees usually cover drawing up the plans and the building specification to submit to the planning authorities as well as supervising the project as it proceeds. The building specification should itemise all the materials to be used, as well as describing the size and style of windows and door frames, and providing information about guttering, tiles etc. Inevitably the possible choice of materials

will be more limited than it is in the UK although it is getting better all the time. Now that Southern Cyprus has joined the EU it is likely to gain wider access to products from all over Europe. This may also be the case for the north if the EU eventually rewards it for seeking reunion by lifting sanctions on the import and export of materials.

If you are having trouble finding an architect contact the Cyprus Civil Engineers and Architects Association (☎2275 1221). The website of the Royal Institute of British Architects also lists some Cypriot architects (☎020-7530 5533, www.riba.org). On some projects you may also need the services of a mechanical or electrical engineer, as well as a quantity surveyor and a health and safety consultant. Most architects will have contacts and will be able to draw up a suitable team of professionals for you.

Structural (Civil) Engineers. In Southern Cyprus it is a legal requirement that the architectural design submitted for planning permission must be checked and signed off by a structural engineer, not least because the island lies in an earthquake zone which means that buildings must be specially reinforced. Their fee will be around 1% of the project cost.

Obtaining a Building Permit. Once the building specification has been approved, a building permit should be issued and you pay the appropriate fee (around C£450 in Southern Cyprus). Note that the building permit may require that you complete the work within three years; if you fail to do so you will have to apply all over again.

Getting Building Quotations. Once planning permission has been granted you can start looking for suitable builders to carry out the work. They will study the plans and the spec and tell you how much they think it will cost them to complete the job. Estimates always vary, both for the time it will take to complete the job and for the total cost, so always get more than one. The best way to find a reliable builder is through personal recommendation although you need to be sure that such praise comes from somebody truly independent (i.e. that the builder is not the cousin of the person recommending him!). Get several quotes and remember that the highest won't necessarily guarantee the best results any more than the lowest automatically means that the work

will be second-rate (although usually you get what you pay for). As at home, there are plenty of people seeking casual building work without registering for tax. If you employ one of them and get found out you may face a heavy fine.

You don't have to work with just one builder – sometimes it is better to have a team of specialists undertaking different parts of the work.

As a ballpark figure building a house from scratch is likely to cost from around C£600 to C£900 per square metre (in Southern Cyprus, less in Northern Cyprus), depending on your tastes in finish and fittings. This is on top of the cost of buying the land.

Building Contracts. Your contract with the builder should stipulate the total price for the job and itemise the work required. Make sure that it is clear who is paying the VAT. You will also need to agree a payment schedule with the builder. Often they want to be paid half the money upfront with the balance payable in stages as the work progresses. Try and arrange to hold back part of the payment as insurance against possible building defects which may not become evident until the house has had time to 'settle'.

All the builders you employ should be covered by insurance so that if they go bankrupt midway through the project you will be able to claim compensation.

Work in Progress. In the south it is a legal requirement that a supervising engineer should be present on the building site at all times and they will be able to advise on all health and safety requirements (although these remain your responsibility ultimately). However, it is also advisable to be on site as much as possible yourself so that you can check that the builders actually put in the hours you're paying for. Being on the spot also ensures that if something unexpected crops up it can be sorted out promptly.

In general it is easier to find good building workers in Southern Cyprus than in the north. In the first place there is more chance of finding workers who can speak good English and in the second since rates of pay are better in the south, the best workers from the north tend to gravitate south in search of work. In general, building standards seem to be rising all over the island. However, the pell-mell pace of

development means that some shoddy workmanship is bound to slip through the net. Because of the amount of construction work going on, skilled workers are in short supply and, just as in the UK, builders often take on several jobs at the same time, leading to unanticipated delays. But there are also many reliable, professional builders who will complete the job exactly as you want them to.

Keep in mind that things rarely go exactly to plan, especially if you decide on changes to the original design. You should therefore budget at least 10% over the estimate to cover all eventualities. If you make changes to the original plans get your lawyer to have them added into the contract and signed by you and the builders to avoid problems when payment time comes round.

Note that because Cyprus is in an earthquake zone you are legally required to build new houses using steel reinforcing rods.

Health and Safety Supervisors. Since 2004 it is has been a legal requirement that every building site in Southern Cyprus has a health and safety supervisor assigned to it. Anyone who belongs to the Technical Chamber of Cyprus can act as a supervisor; your architect should be able to advise you.

How to Smooth the Building Process

- As everywhere, builders can be unreliable. Try to be on site as much as possible. Failing that, employ someone to keep an eye on things for you. Ask them to send you photographic updates of the work as it goes along.
- Make sure that the building materials listed in the specification are the ones you want and not those that the builder can pick up cheaply.
- Stagger payments to the builders and hold back final payment until some time after completion so that if any problems appear (e.g. cracks in the walls or drainage difficulties) you will have some leverage to persuade them to come back and do the repairs.
- Depending on its size and design expect to have to wait up to a year before you can gaze upon your dream house. Even after completion it could take another year or so to finish the landscaping.

Completion. After the house has been finished and the architect has signed the Payment Certificate you will need to make your final payments. You will also need to make a declaration which will allow you to add the new building to the original title deed relating to the land.

Because a lot of foreigners are interested in building their own house, some agents and developers have started to buy up plots of land and obtain the necessary permits ahead of time so that they are ready to sell on to suitable clients. Some developers also sell plots in their housing schemes for individuals to build their own house on.

DIY. If you are good at DIY you will be at a considerable advantage when it comes to building a house from scratch. Not only will you be able to save some money by doing some of the work yourself but you will also be better able to assess the quality of the workmanship and foresee problems before they occur. So if you think you might want to self-build, your pre-retirement plans should certainly include taking courses at night school in such useful subjects as plumbing, wiring and carpentry.

Sandy Wiley is building a brand-new house on land near Polis.

'Twenty years ago I would probably have bought in France but I came on a three-day inspection visit to Pafos, came to Polis and found this land which already had planning permission. The developer was able to recommend an architect. She had trained in Budapest and we are so happy with her. We discuss our ideas with her and then she interprets them to suit the land. Both the builder and the architect have become our good friends now.'

Once the building is complete (which is often 18 months to two years from the application for building consent) the architect must apply to the planning authorities for a **certificate of final approval** (basically, their agreement that the building matches what had been permitted).

Building Contacts in Cyprus

Erozan Mimarlık Mühendislik Bürosu: 15 Namık Kemal Meydanı, Suriçi, Gazimağusa; ☎ 366 4882.

Arch Property Development & Construction Company: 67 Ziya Rızkı Caddesi, Girne, Mersin 10; ☎ 0392-815 8709; alkin@arch-cyprus-properties.com.

THE PURCHASING PROCEDURE

First off, the good news. Since Cypriot law is based on British law the buying process will seem fairly familiar wherever you live on the island. Then the bad news. So much development has taken place on the island in recent years that there is a small chance of encountering sharks either amongst the estate agents or the builders. It is also especially important to understand the political situation in Cyprus and the impact that it has had on who owns what (see below).

Approval to Buy

Since 2004 resident EU citizens no longer need approval from the Council of Ministers before they can buy property in **Southern Cyprus**. However, all non-resident non-Cypriots still have to seek approval to buy. Getting approval is normally very straightforward provided that you don't have a criminal record at home or in Cyprus and can show that you can support yourself – the Ministers normally assume that a couple need around C£12,000 to support themselves. However, you may have to wait a long time for the approval to come through. In the unlikely event that approval is refused after you have completed the purchase of your property you can reapply to the Council, resell the house or try and persuade the vendor to reimburse you.

In **Northern Cyprus** you need a purchase permit from the Council of Ministers, a process that can take anything from four to 18 months because of the current backlog of applications (although attempts are currently being made to speed things up). If you use a public notary to make your application it should cost around £750; if you use a lawyer it will probably cost around £1,500.

Why the Title Deed is Especially Important in Cyprus

Because of Cyprus's complicated political situation it is important to be very sure about the exact legal situation of the property you are interested in, especially in **Northern Cyprus**. It is vital to see the title deed (*koçan, tapu*) of the property and to check the number in the lower right-hand corner. If it has 'TRNC' written in front of it you should proceed with caution since it means that the property has been given to its current 'owner' by the northern Cypriot government, either

as a reward for a period of military service or because they are settlers from the mainland. As many as 85% of new developments in Northern Cyprus may be on TRNC-titled properties. It is unclear what will happen to these places once a final settlement is reached.

Estate agents' adverts sometimes claim that a property has an original Turkish or Greek (or even British) title deed which sounds promising. However, the Northern Cyprus government makes it difficult for such properties to be sold to foreigners, fearing that soon there will be no reasonably-priced and legally secure properties available for local people to buy.

TITLE DEEDS

The peculiar circumstances of Cyprus mean that what is written on the title deed is even more important than normal. There are four different types of title deed (*koçan* or *tapu* in Turkish):

- Freehold title deeds issued to Greek or Turkish Cypriots before 1974. These are unlikely to be challenged in the future. In the north the government restricts foreign ownership of these properties.
- Freehold title deeds issued to British or other foreign owners before 1974. These are also uncontentious.
- Untitled land which belonged to Greeks or Turks before 1974. If no title deed exists, precise ownership of the land is obviously questionable.
- So-called TRNC title deeds. These have been issued for properties that belonged to Greeks before 1974 and which were exchanged for land in the south in the settlement after the invasion (exchanged land is called *eşdeğer* land in Turkish). Some people believe these deeds are legally precarious. Similar deeds exist in the south too but in the north the government often gave them out as rewards to Turkish soldiers and settlers whose legal entitlement to stay in the north – let alone to sell the properties – is debatable.

In **Southern Cyprus** land that was owned by Turkish Cypriots is usually only rented out or used for short-term purposes. However, there have

been cases where such land has been sold by unscrupulous individuals, a recent case in point being land in Dillirga. In another case the Greek Cypriot government has confiscated Turkish Cypriot land to build a power station on it. There are those who argue that even Larnaka airport has been built on what is rightfully Turkish Cypriot land.

Unfortunately it is not always easy to get estate agents and developers to let you see the title deed at the start of the buying process. However, wherever possible you should certainly try to see it even if it means a trip to the Land Registry Office in Lefkosia or the Land Registry and Surveying Office in Lefkoşa.

Overview of the Purchasing Procedure

Since Cypriot law is based on British law, the ins and outs of the buying process can seem superficially similar to those in the UK both in the north and the south. However, there are subtle differences and, as a foreigner, you may be less attuned to the nuances of what is going on, so it's as well to start with a step-by-step guide to buying a property in **Southern Cyprus**:

Step 1 – Choose an Estate Agent, Consult a Lawyer and Find your Ideal Property. How to find an estate agent has already been dealt with above. Nevertheless, it is worth reiterating the importance of finding a reputable agent. It is also a good idea to have a lawyer on board as soon as possible since they will need to make a written request to the Council of Ministers for you to be allowed to buy a property. The importance of finding a reliable and impartial lawyer is covered below. Whether you choose a local or UK-based lawyer, you should make sure that they are fluent in both Greek or Turkish and English, and are fully versed in the minutiae of the local legal and tax regimes.

Step 2 – Make an Offer. Having found a property and decided how to pay for it (see the *Housing Finance* chapter) you should put in an offer to the estate agent. Once it is accepted, you will have to pay a small reservation fee (usually non-refundable). Your lawyer will then show the Exchange Control Officer proof that you are paying for the property with foreign currency.

Step 3 – Carry out Surveys, Sign the Contract and Pay the Deposit. If you are buying a resale property, your lawyer should start negotiating the contract. Meanwhile any surveys and legal checks should be carried out. When you sign

the contract you will have to transfer a deposit of between 10% and 30% of the price. The date of completion should be agreed in this contract. If you pull out of the sale after signing this agreement you will lose your deposit. At this point the property is taken off the market and the contract must be registered with the Land Registry Office within 60 days. From this time no one can resell or remortgage the property to anyone else – gazumping and gazundering are not normal in Cyprus.

If you are buying an off-plan property, you will have to sign a contract agreeing to make staged payments as building work advances. Ensure that you have the full building specification for the property translated into English, together with copies of the agreements you have signed.

Step 4 – Completion. Once all the final checks have been made you will need to transfer the balance of the selling price to be able to take possession of the property. With a resale property full payment will usually be required within 30 days. If you are buying an off-plan project you may pay several staged installments and only pay the balance once the building is complete. Transfer of the deeds will then be registered with the Land Registry – it is the buyer's responsibility to ensure that this has been done. Note that there are routinely very long delays (up to five years) before the title deed becomes available. This does not prevent you moving into the house once payment is complete. You do not have to pay the transfer fees until the deeds are issued even if this takes several years – the sum due will be calculated according to the property's value on the day you originally agreed to buy it provided you deposited the sales contract at the Land Registry at the time.

Procedures are very similar in **Northern Cyprus**. There you usually put down a sum of about £1,000 to get the ball rolling. Your lawyer will then start carrying out the necessary background checks to make sure that there are no problems with the property you want to buy. Once these have been completed the lawyer informs the government and the police start checks to ensure that you don't have a criminal record. Once they are satisfied you pay a deposit and the sale then proceeds much as it does in the south. It is quite normal to move into your house without having a copy of the title deed because of delays at the Land Registry which is not yet computerised (a recent survey found that there were 3,900 title deeds awaiting completion).

Lawyers

Although many locals don't use a lawyer when buying a property, it is very important that you, as a foreigner, employ an independent lawyer to look after your interests. Theoretically you could try and find a lawyer working with a specialist law firm in the UK. However, in practice there are few companies with a specialist interest in Cyprus. At the very least you should try and find an English-speaking Cypriot lawyer to avoid the risk of linguistic hiccoughs.

As well as guiding you through the legal processes involved in buying your property, the lawyer should be able to:

- Advise on whose name the property should be registered in as this can have important consequences as regards taxation.
- Advise on how to pay for the property (through a mortgage or re-mortgage, in cash, by forming a company etc.) and on how to minimise costs.
- Arrange a power of attorney, if needed (see below).
- Arrange for the signing of the contract and for payment in instalments.
- Check that there are no problems because proper planning permission was not obtained when the property was originally built.
- Draw up contracts between you and a builder and/or architect.
- Look after the conveyancing.
- Pay taxes and other fees on your behalf.

If you use a Cypriot lawyer they may be unfamiliar with UK law and the effect that buying a property overseas can have on your tax or legal situation back home. Also, bear in mind that Cypriot lawyers tend to specialise in individual areas of law, so you should make sure that you hire a lawyer who is an expert in property law and knows a lot about the market you're interested in. For example, a lawyer who is only used to dealing with coastal villas may not have the same expertise when it comes to buying a rural ruin.

> Be wary of using the services of a lawyer recommended by an estate agent as their impartiality may be compromised. Lawyers who are not fully independent may be tempted to draw up contracts in the interests of the agency they work with. What's more you may not be able to rely on them to fight your corner wholeheartedly if a dispute arises.

If you know very little Greek or Turkish you should definitely find a lawyer who speaks English. Local lawyers will be used to dealing with foreigners and sometimes advertise their services in the English-language press.

The lawyer should be able to identify any outstanding bills attached to the property and ensure that you are indemnified against having to pay them. They should also check with the Land Registry that the title deed is in order and that the property has proper road access in which case securing planning permission for development is virtually guaranteed.

If you want to buy property with land attached to it, your lawyer should be able to find out about planning restrictions and local by-laws concerning water, grazing or hunting, and land access rights. You may also want your lawyer to check where the property boundaries start and end as what the owners say may not coincide with what is recorded on the deed. If you are buying into an apartment block you may also want the rules and regulations checked by a lawyer.

It is wise to find a lawyer before starting your house-hunting since they will be able to warn you about possible pitfalls. They will also be ready to look at draft contracts – you may be able to fax them over while you are in Cyprus and wait for advice before committing yourself to something you might later regret.

Fees. Some lawyers will agree a percentage of the price (usually around 1-1.5% of the purchase price), while others charge on an hourly basis or take a flat fee; it is always best to start by asking for an explanation of the fees and an estimate of the hours involved. The cost will inevitably rise if extra clauses have to be added to a standard contract or if there are lengthy negotiations over the price. If you are taking out a mortgage this may involve correspondence between the solicitors and the mortgage company. This, too, will bump up the price.

If you are buying off-plan, the lawyer will generally charge around

1% of the property value plus an hourly rate for work done on your behalf while construction continues. Because there can never be an absolutely firm completion date, more work may need to be done as the project unfolds. The lawyer should be able to give you an estimate of the likely cost once they have looked at the existing paperwork.

Finding a Lawyer

It is best to find a lawyer through personal recommendation. Failing that there are a number of alternatives. In the UK the *Law Society* (☎020-7242 1222; www.lawsoc.org.uk) holds lists of Law Society-registered English-speaking lawyers in Cyprus; the website allows you to search for lawyers who specialise in residential conveyancing. Cypriot consulates and embassies will also hold lists of English-speaking lawyers (for their contact details see Embassies & Consulates in Chapter 2: *Basics*).

UK-Based Lawyers

Bennett & Co Solicitors: ☎01625-586937; www.bennett-and-co.com; 144 Knutsford Road, Wilmslow, Cheshire SK9 6JP.

John Howell & Co: ☎020 7420 0400; www.lawoverseas.com; The Old Glassworks, 22 Endell Street, Covent Garden, London WC2H 9AD.

The International Property Law Centre: Suffolk House, 21 Silver Street, Hull HU1 1JG; ☎0870 800 4565; fax 0870 800 4567; e-mail internationalproperty@maxgold.com; www.internationalpropertylaw.com. Specialists in the purchase and sale of property and businesses in Cyprus, with in-house foreign lawyers. Fixed quote and no VAT payable. Contact Stefano Lucatello, Senior Partner (☎0870 800 4565, e-mail stefanol@maxgold.com).

Vahib & Co Solicitors: ☎020-8348 0055; www.vahib.co.uk; 435 Green Lanes, Haringey, London N4 1HA.

Cypriot Lawyers

Andreas Demetriades & Co: ☎2681 1668; Pafos.

Cyprus Legal Service: ☎2244 1722; leontiou@logosnet.cy.net; Lefkosia.

Hasan Balman: P.K. 552, 6 Ankara Sokak, Lefkosa Mersin 10; ☎0392 227 5868; e-mail hasan@cypruspropertylawyer.com.

Gölboy Göryel: 26-28 Cumhuriyet Caddesi, Girne, Mersin 10; ☎0392 815 2097; e-mail gulboy@cypruspropertylawyer.com.

Proact Partnership: ☎2681 9424, www.proactpartnership.com.

It is common to be asked to put up some of the money when the lawyer starts work; the remainder will be due on completion of the purchase. A cheap lawyer in either part of the island will do your conveyancing for about £500 but a more reputable one is likely to ask closer to £1,000-£1,300.

Checks and Surveys

Before buying a piece of land to build on you should ask to see the title deeds. If that is not possible you should still find out the reference number for the piece of land at the Land Registry where you can check the plans. In particular you should look to see what zoning the land has (e.g. is it registered as agricultural or industrial land?). You should also check the status of adjacent plots of land since what your neighbours do can have a dramatic effect on how happy you are in your new home. While in the planning department you can also check how much of the land you can build on and whether there are any restrictions on how many floors you can have.

If you see the letters 'A.M' on the map it means that your property is near an ancient monument in which case you need to check that the Antiquities Department will not object to your building on the land. If your land falls within 90m of the sea you may find that you can't build on it.

From the plans you should also be able to check that there is access to your property. If the nearest public road is more than 180m from it you will probably be refused permission to build.

In theory you should always have any property that you are thinking of buying professionally surveyed. However, surveying a property before buying it is not the norm in Cyprus and many people buy on sight alone. Inevitably there are horror stories about people who bought a flat that looked fine, only to find that it became flooded in winter; or who found that a seemingly unimportant hairline crack is expanding year by year. If you need a mortgage to buy the property, the lenders will probably require a valuation if not a full survey, to confirm that the property is worth the purchase price.

A valuation report is likely to cost you at least C£150 and a full survey C£200 in Southern Cyprus.

When you first view a property, look for obvious signs of subsidence, bowing walls, damp patches or strange smells. Check for dry rot (stick a knife into windowsills and other areas where damp is likely to strike), a leaking roof (stains on the ceilings), and cracks or fractures in the walls. Be on the look out for signs of rising damp or condensation/ humidity. Check that the plumbing, wiring and heating systems are in good working order, as well as that the drainage and water provision are trouble-free. If there is a well on the land ask if it has been tested recently. Take your time and get the feel of the place – you will usually be able to tell if there are major structural problems.

Surveys. A trained surveyor will be able to prepare a detailed report on the property for around £1,000-£1,500 depending on its size. Be sure to get any such report translated into English.

Because of differences in surveying criteria you should make sure that you know what you want checked and discuss this with the surveyor. Few vendors will sign a contract of sale with a 'subject to survey' clause; if someone else comes along before you are happy about the property's soundness, you will probably lose out on the chance to buy.

Finding a Surveyor

The Royal Institute of Chartered Surveyors' website has a directory (www.ricsfirms.com) of 18 member organisations in Cyprus; search by location to find the company nearest to you. Alternatively look in the Classified ads section of the local English-language newspaper.

Expert Opinions. If you're still uncertain, you could arrange for a local estate agent (other than the one showing you the property) to offer their opinion. Alternatively a local builder may be able to advise on the property's structural soundness and whether the asking price is realistic. If you intend to buy a property for renovation you will need to get quotes from several builders anyway. These opinions may cost you money but it will have been well spent if it sets your mind at rest.

Contracts and Conveyancing

Most contracts of sale used in Cyprus are standard documents with gaps to be filled in. Yours will be drawn up by an estate agent or developer or, if you decide to buy privately from an individual, by the vendor's lawyer. If it is for a new building it should be based on the model contracts drawn up by The Joint Committee of Architects, Engineers, Quantity Surveyors and Building Contractors of Cyprus, which is, in turn, based on British models, and should cover the agreed price, the work to be done and the time it is expected to take. Even if it is a standard contract you should ensure that your lawyer has checked it before you sign and if there are clauses that bother you, you must insist that they are renegotiated even if this increases your legal costs. If you are buying a property that is incomplete it is common for the contract to contain a clause requiring the builder to put up a 10% performance bond, a bank guarantee against his going bankrupt before the work is complete.

The building boom means that Cyprus is becoming more of a buyers' market and you should never let yourself be rushed into signing anything – it is better to lose almost any property than buy something which turns out to be wrong for you. Never sign anything without taking independent legal advice first; if there is a real reason why you must move fast, then at least fax a copy of the contract to your legal representatives. In Southern Cyprus contracts are written in English although in the north they are in Turkish.

> There may be tax advantages as well as financial savings to be made at a later stage if you register the property in the joint names of a wife and husband, in the name of your children, in the name of the person who will inherit the property, or in the name of a limited company. You will need good legal advice to ascertain which arrangement is best for you.

In **Southern Cyprus** you should file your contract of sale with the District Land Registry within 60 days even if you do not yet have the title deed. If you do this it will be extremely difficult for the seller to change their mind in the interim; if you do not then you would only be able to claim damages if they do something tricky like remortgaging the property.

It is not essential to stay in Cyprus while the purchase process is being completed. Instead you can sign a power of attorney which will allow a solicitor to act on your behalf. If you arrange this power of attorney from the UK, it will need to be witnessed and stamped by a public notary (something like a legal clerk) in Cyprus.

Jeremy Hall had a word of warning for would-be buyers in **Northern Cyprus:** '*Contracts with builders and so on are effectively unenforceable. But they* will *be enforced against a buyer.*' Of course local estate agents deny that this is the case.

Contracts For Off-Plan Purchases. If you are buying off-plan, the schedule for making the stage payments should be clearly set out in the contract; it is better to have them tied to the completion of specific stages of the building work rather than to specific dates which might give the builder an incentive to work more slowly. It is also advisable to negotiate a clause that permits you to withhold perhaps 10% of the cost price for a defined time after you have moved into the property as a guarantee against possible defects. This will ensure that the builders come back to rectify any problems.

A typical payment schedule might look like this:

- On signing the contract: 20% deposit.
- On completion of a set phase in the building work (e.g. completion of the exterior walls and roof): 25% of the agreed purchase price.
- On completion of another phase in the building work (e.g. completion of interior): Another 25% of the agreed purchase price.
- On completion of project: Outstanding balance less anything held back until you are sure there are no problems.

Questions to Ask Before Completion

Resale Properties

- Has your solicitor checked that the vendor is the legally registered owner of the property?
- Has a survey been carried out to your satisfaction?
- Are fittings and/or furniture included in the purchase price?

- Are there planning restrictions which might stop you altering the property?
- Have there been any alterations that have not been registered with the authorities?
- Will you have to pay community charges? How much are local taxes?
- Has your solicitor checked that the property is free of debts or charges; that all bills have been paid; and that all taxes are up to date? Remember that debts attached to a property are 'inherited' by the new owner, however unfair that may seem.
- Are there restrictions on the uses that can be made of the property?
- Are the boundaries, access and any public rights of way clearly defined?
- Have you checked the town plan to make sure there are no future developments (e.g. building projects) that might affect the property's value or your view?
- Have you checked the description of the property in the Land Registry to make sure it coincides with what you think you are buying?

Further Checks For Off-Plan or New-Build Properties

- Do the developers/builders hold the necessary planning permission to build on the land?
- Have you seen a full description of the materials, fixtures and fittings they will be using?
- Are you clear what you are paying for? Will the surrounding ground be landscaped? What will the property look like when complete?
- Are the payment schedule and completion date clear?
- Have you protected yourself against the possibility of the developers going bankrupt before the work is finished?
- Has the property been registered with the local authorities for real estate taxes?

Further Checks For Buying Land to Build On

- Will you be able to get a building permit?
- How much will it cost to build on the land and can you afford the costs?

- Is there unrestricted access to the land?
- If the utilities (electricity, gas, water, phone) are not already running to the plot are you sure that you will be able to get them installed at a realistic price?

Fees

It is probably wise to assume that the cost of arranging to buy your property will amount to around 10% of the purchase price. The cheaper the property the more likely it is that a higher percentage will apply because of minimum charges imposed by lawyers and others involved in the conveyancing.

SUMMARY OF TYPICAL CONVEYANCING COSTS FOR NEW PROPERTY IN SOUTHERN CYPRUS

- Lawyer's conveyancing fee: varies depending on the property but perhaps £300 for a small apartment in Paralimni and closer to £1,200 for a three-bedroomed house in Pafos.
- Property Transfer Fee: 3% up to C£50,000; 5% between C£50,000 and C£100,000; and 8% from C£100,000 upwards. If two people buy in joint names they can each take advantage of these bandings which reduces the bill.
- Stamp Duty: 1.5% up to C£100,000, then 2% for remainder.
- VAT: 5% for first-time buyers and principle places of residence, 15% for everyone else.

Property Transfer Fees & Purchase Tax. In **Southern Cyprus** house purchasers must pay a transfer fee of 3% on properties worth up to C£50,000. Between C£50,000 and C£100,000 the rate rises to 5%, and from C£100,000 upwards it becomes 8%. These rates apply to each person separately, so if a husband and wife buy a house in their joint names they can reduce their tax bill.

In **Northern Cyprus**, house purchasers must pay 3% purchase tax. This tax is levied according to the Land Registry valuation which is likely to be lower than the actual purchase price as it excludes fixtures and fittings.

Stamp Duty. When the time comes to sign the contract in **Southern Cyprus** you will have to pay Stamp Duty at a rate of C£1.50 per C£1000 up to C£100,000 and then C£2.00 per C£1,000 from C£100,000 upwards. This must be paid within 30 days or you will incur a fine. **Northern Cyprus** has no stamp duty.

Land Registry Fees. For **Southern Cyprus** you must pay a minimal fee of C£1 for depositing your contract at the Land Registry.

EXAMPLE OF COSTS INVOLVED IN PURCHASE OF A NEW-BUILD C£150,000 PROPERTY IN SOUTHERN CYPRUS	
Reservation fee	C£1,000
Legal fees	C£1,000
Stamp duty	C£200
Property transfer fee	C£8,000
VAT (5%)	C£7,500
TOTAL	**C£17,700**

KDV/VAT. In **Northern Cyprus** you must pay 5% KDV (VAT) on all house purchases. In **Southern Cyprus** you pay 5% VAT on a new building that is to be your principle place of residence. However, if the building is to be a second home you will be liable for 15% VAT. Building plots are exempt from VAT until 2007 as are buildings that received their building permits before 1 May 2004. First-time buyers pay a lower rate of 5% VAT on their purchases although usually they have to pay the 15% and then reclaim 10%!

SUMMARY OF TYPICAL CONVEYANCING COSTS FOR PROPERTY IN NORTHERN CYPRUS

- Lawyer's conveyancing fee: varies depending on the property but averages £1,000.
- Purchase Tax: 6%, payable on transfer of deed which may be years after sale is completed. For a first purchase the tax is only 3%.
- KDV: 5%.

EXAMPLE OF COSTS INVOLVED IN PURCHASE OF A £55,000 PROPERTY IN NORTHERN CYPRUS	
Legal fees	£1,000
KDV	£2,750
Purchase Tax	£1,650
TOTAL	**£5,400**

Other Probable Costs

- The estate agent's fee is likely to be around 3% of the purchase price. If a UK agent's representative has been involved their fee should be included in the overall agent's fee.
- Surveyors' fees depend on the type of survey carried out (valuation only, full structural survey etc).
- Connection fees may have to be paid if a new property lacks water, electricity or a telephone. There will probably be a charge for changing the name on utility bills to your own.
- Mortgage and mortgage arrangement fees.
- Contents and building insurance.
- Charges for transferring funds from a UK bank account to a Cypriot bank account.

The Land Registry Offices

All land transfers are recorded in the Land Registry Offices in Lefkosia and Lefkoşa respectively. These Land Registry Offices keep details of the size and location of every property as well as of its value and its current ownership. The Land Registry Office in Northern Cyprus has come under particular strain in the last few years, with 15 civil servants struggling to process more than 7,000 applications for land measurements in 2005 alone. The office is currently being computerised and more staff are being taken on. However, delays can seem interminable when you are waiting for information; without a solicitor to help you they are likely to be even worse. Eventually you will need to go to the Land Registry Office to sign the title deed and

complete its transfer into your name. Take your passport with you as identification when you go.

Traditionally the price declared on title deeds was much lower than the actual price paid for a property in a conscious effort to reduce the tax owed. However, under-declaring the price of a property is illegal unless you are doing so because you have a separate agreement to cover the cost of fixtures and fittings. Doing so will also mean that if you decide to sell the property at a later date the increase in value of the property will be disproportionately large and you will face a larger capital gains tax bill. Now that Southern Cyprus has joined the EU it is likely that such glitches will slowly be eradicated. However, in North Cyprus it will be some time yet before people routinely admit what they paid for a property.

District Land Registry Offices

Ammochostos: ☎2430 4288; 59 Faneromenis St, Larnaka.
Larnaka: ☎2480 3301, 6 Medousis St.
Lefkosia: ☎2230 3939; 21 Acheon St/10 Etolon St.
Lemesos: ☎2580 4800; Franklin Roosevolt Ave.
Pafos: ☎2680 2300; 44 Eleftheriou Venizelou St.
Paralimni: ☎2382 1253; 26A Marias Siniklitikis St.

Completion

The date that completion is due to take place should be written into your contact although it may slip depending on such problems as your lawyer discovering unpaid taxes secured against the property. If you are buying a resale property completion should take place no later than two or three months after signing the initial agreement to buy; if you are buying off-plan completion may not happen until a year or so has passed.

Get your lawyer to read a draft copy of the final contract carefully. Then make a last check on the property to see that everything is in order and that all the fixtures and fittings that were meant to be included in the price remain in place.

Once everything has been settled you sign the contract, as does the vendor (or a lawyer representing the vendor) and that is that.

If the property is ready for immediate occupation you make your final payment at this time. You will only have to pay the property transfer fee/purchase tax when the title deed becomes available which may be long after you move in.

In **Southern Cyprus** the actual transfer of ownership takes place at the District Land Registry office. Here you will need to show:

- Your permission to buy signed by the Council of Ministers.
- A certificate from the Central Bank confirming that you paid for the property with foreign currency.
- Receipts to show that all tax and utility payments are up to date.
- Your passport.

At this point the District Land Officer will check the value of the property to determine how much transfer tax is due. They are free to challenge the price given in the contract if it is at odds with the valuation given in the Land Registry. However, it is increasingly rare for the buyer to receive the title deed promptly; indeed, there are now case of people who have been waiting up to 15 years without receiving the deeds.

Specific Performance

This strange-sounding law requires both parties to the sales contract to carry out their part of the agreement. It is possible that it could be invoked by purchasers who have found themselves waiting interminably for their title deed to be transferred. To start proceedings against the vendor you would have to give notice in writing that you expected them to fulfil their side of the contract and then wait six months before proceeding to law. So far, though, no one appears to be doing this.

Problems

Although most people experience no problems with their purchases on either side of the island some, especially those buying in Northern Cyprus, have had less satisfactory experiences. There was, for example, the notorious case of Gary Robb, a British property developer whose company, Aga Developments, had started work on 400 houses at Amaranta Valley in Arapköy (TRNC) in 2005 when Robb fled to

Thailand with much of the company's capital. At the time of writing he had offered to return and finish the buildings despite being stripped of his citizenship; faced with the expense of finishing off the buildings the government was at least considering his offer. More common experiences have included discovering that the builder has not obtained the necessary permits before starting work or has mortgaged the land while the work was in progress; being faced with demands for extra payments to install utilities at the last moment; and long delays in the transfer of title deeds.

To help them pool their experiences and find redress for their problems a group of British settlers in Northern Cyprus have set up the Homebuyers Pressure Group (www.homebuyerspressuregroup.com). Log on for clues as to what warning signs to look out for.

But it would be a mistake to believe all the problems occur in the north. With between 600 and 700 property developers hard at work in the south there are bound to be some whose work doesn't come up to scratch as well as some downright cowboys. Some of the latter have been known to start work without planning permission and use the property they are supposedly selling as collateral against their own loans. The watchword has to be buyer beware.

A virtually routine problem in the south is the delay in issuing the title deed. Sometimes this is because the building boom means that the Land Registry has a backlog of deeds to deal with but sometimes it is because the construction company is holding back on releasing the deeds. There can be many reasons for this, not least that the more property they 'own', the better their balance sheet looks. If you suspect this to be the case ask the builder if the Certificate of Building Approval has been issued; if it has then they really should be able to transfer ownership to you. In theory you could sue the builder for failure in Specific Performance of the contract. However, this assumes that the title deed actually exists which it may not in a building complex where the plot has to be subdivided and deeds prepared for each plot. Provided you have used an independent lawyer and have registered your sales contract at the Land Registry the fact that you have no title deed shouldn't cause you too many sleepless nights. There is rarely any problem in reselling a property in these circumstances.

RENOVATING A PROPERTY

Buying an old building in need of renovation should be approached with extreme caution. You need to be sure that you have the know-how to renovate a ruin or that you have the funds to pay builders to do the work for you; depending on the amount of work involved, buying a property to renovate can work out at least one-third more expensive than buying a new-build.

However much you may want to restore an existing building, very often the only realistic option is to demolish the existing structure, keep the old stones and then rebuild, using the stones as a facing. This is because many old village properties were built of stone and mud-brick and rarely have decent drains, a damp-proof course or wiring that meets modern needs.

In spite of that, few things can be more satisfying than bringing a derelict property back to life again. Russ Douglas from Birmingham has spent the best part of four years restoring an old farm property near Polis.

> *We found it on the day we were due to fly home,' he says. 'And it was love at first sight. Of course we've had our troubles with builders but I could do some of the work myself. At the moment we're living in the stable although the house is almost ready to move into. Every time I pull up in front of it I just think I must be the luckiest man in the world.*

> **Permission to Renovate**
> Even if you want to renovate an existing building, you will need to get a building permit from the local planning authorities. Before buying a property in need of renovation make sure that both the vendor and their solicitor know that you will only buy it subject to the granting of planning permission. A building permit will probably cost around 4% of the total cost of renovation.

For information about finding builders and the building process, see *Having a House Built from Scratch* earlier in this chapter.

Precautions to Take When Buying Old Properties

- Get a structural survey done before signing a contract. Renovation may turn out to be completely unrealistic and demolition the only option in which case you need to know that the planning authorities will allow this.
- Find out about planning regulations from the local council. You need to know whether you will be allowed to extend the existing building or only to renovate it to its original design. If you are buying in a village or in an old town centre conservation laws may apply to all older properties.
- Obtaining the title deeds (*koçan*) can be particularly difficult in rural areas. In the villages some legitimate property claims have never been formally recognised with title deeds. In this case a court decision may be needed to establish the property's rightful owner in which case it may be better not to continue with the purchase.
- It is more common to discover that what it says on the title deed doesn't correspond with what is being offered for sale. Such problems can usually be resolved but you must make sure that everything is finalised before you buy. Once the property is legally yours, so will any ensuing aggro be yours!
- Get your lawyer to check that there are no debts attached to the property. Under Cypriot law the new owner becomes liable for any unpaid debts.

Grants. At the time of writing government grants were available for restoring old properties in **Southern Cyprus**. In order to take advantage of the scheme you need to find a property that can become a listed building. Once you have had it listed you then apply for planning permission to restore (expect a delay of up to a year before this comes through). You may then be eligible for a grant of up to 40% of the cost of restoration up to a total of C£40,000. For more information either speak to an architect or to someone in the planning department.

Useful Contact

Bettabilt Services Ltd: ☎2693 5839, www.bettabilt.com; Pafos. Specialists in restoring old properties.